FOREWORD

Dear Reader,

From the little treasures in your own backyard, to the vast landscapes peppered across our beautiful land, your favourite wildlife wonders and special people, places and memories that hold great significance. Each and every one of us feels a unique piece of Australia in our hearts. These talented artists share their own stories through words and pictures, and we encourage you to do the same.

What's in your Australian heArt?

Romi Sharp, Just Write For Kids Australia

A percentage of proceeds from this book will be donated to
THE INDIGENOUS LITERACY FOUNDATION
to support literacy learning in remote Aboriginal and Torres Strait Islander communities.
Visit indigenousliteracyfoundation.org.au.

ACKNOWLEDGEMENT OF COUNTRY

We acknowledge the Traditional Custodians of Country throughout Australia and their connections to land, sea and community. We pay our respects to their Elders past and present and extend that respect to all Aboriginal and Torres Strait Islander peoples.

First published by Daisy Lane Publishing 2023
In collaboration with Just Write For Kids Australia 2023

Cover image © Rachael Robertson 2023
Printed in Australia.

© Daisy Lane Publishing
www.daisylanepublishing.com
© Just Write For Kids Australia
www.justkidslit.com

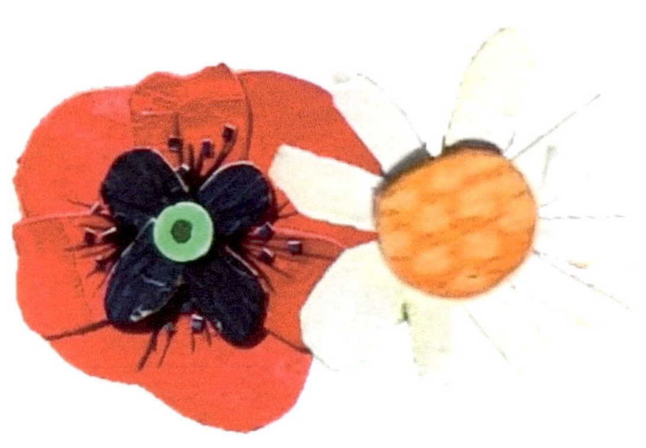
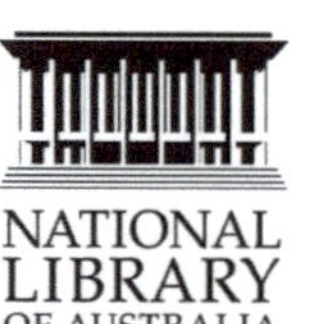

National Library of Australia Cataloguing in-Publication entry
ISBN: (HC) 9780645842722
ISBN: (SC) 9780645842739

Just Write For Kids Australia and Friends

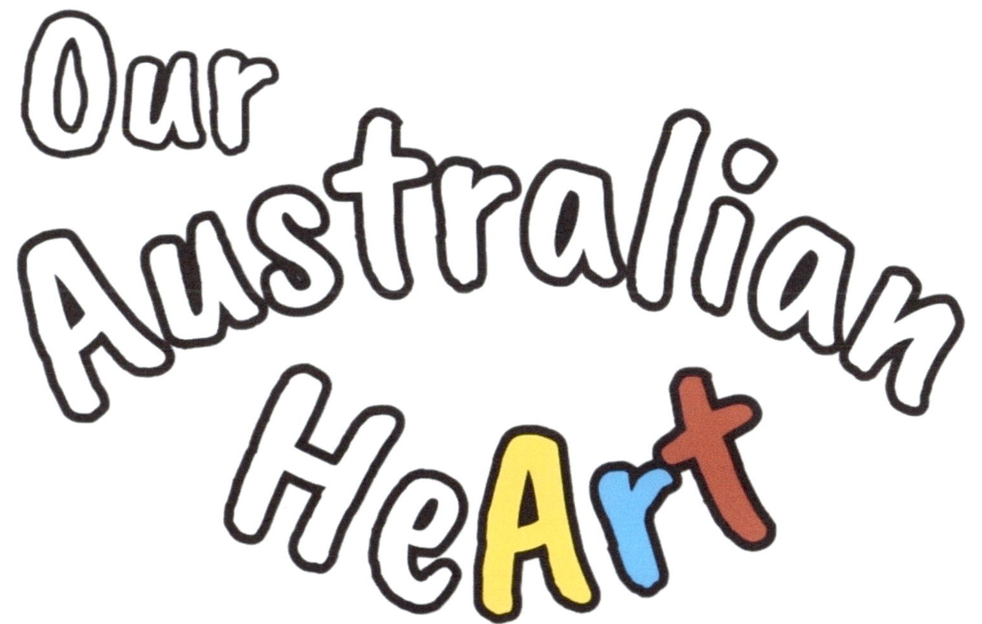

Our Australian HeArt

Bridget Acreman - Suzanne Barton - Mel Corrigan - Kim de Haan - Michèle Dodd - Alisha Dyer - Naomi Eccles-Smith - Hannah Friend - Daniela Glyntzos - Imogen Hartland - Jacqui Hewlett - Carla Hoffenberg - Jennifer Horn - Jessica Miller - Lorraine Miller - Rhonda Ooi - Rachael Robertson - Jeanette Stampone

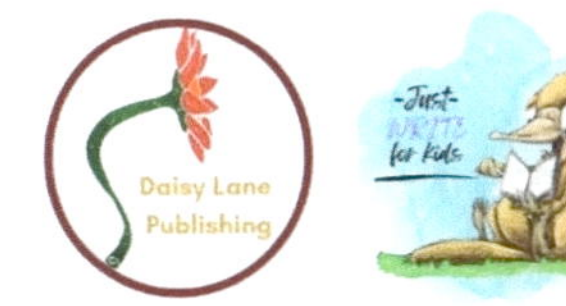

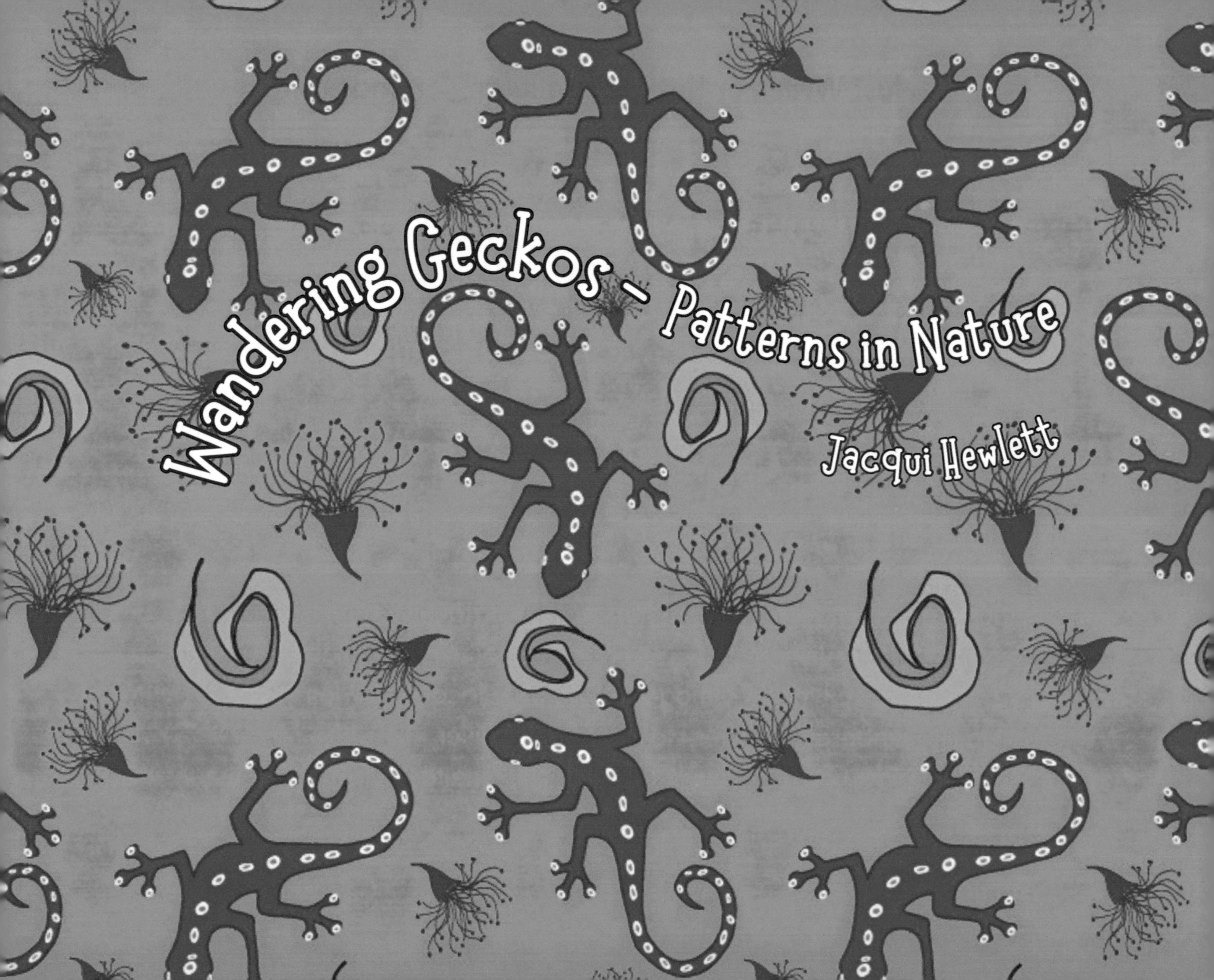

Wandering Geckos – Patterns in Nature
Jacqui Hewlett

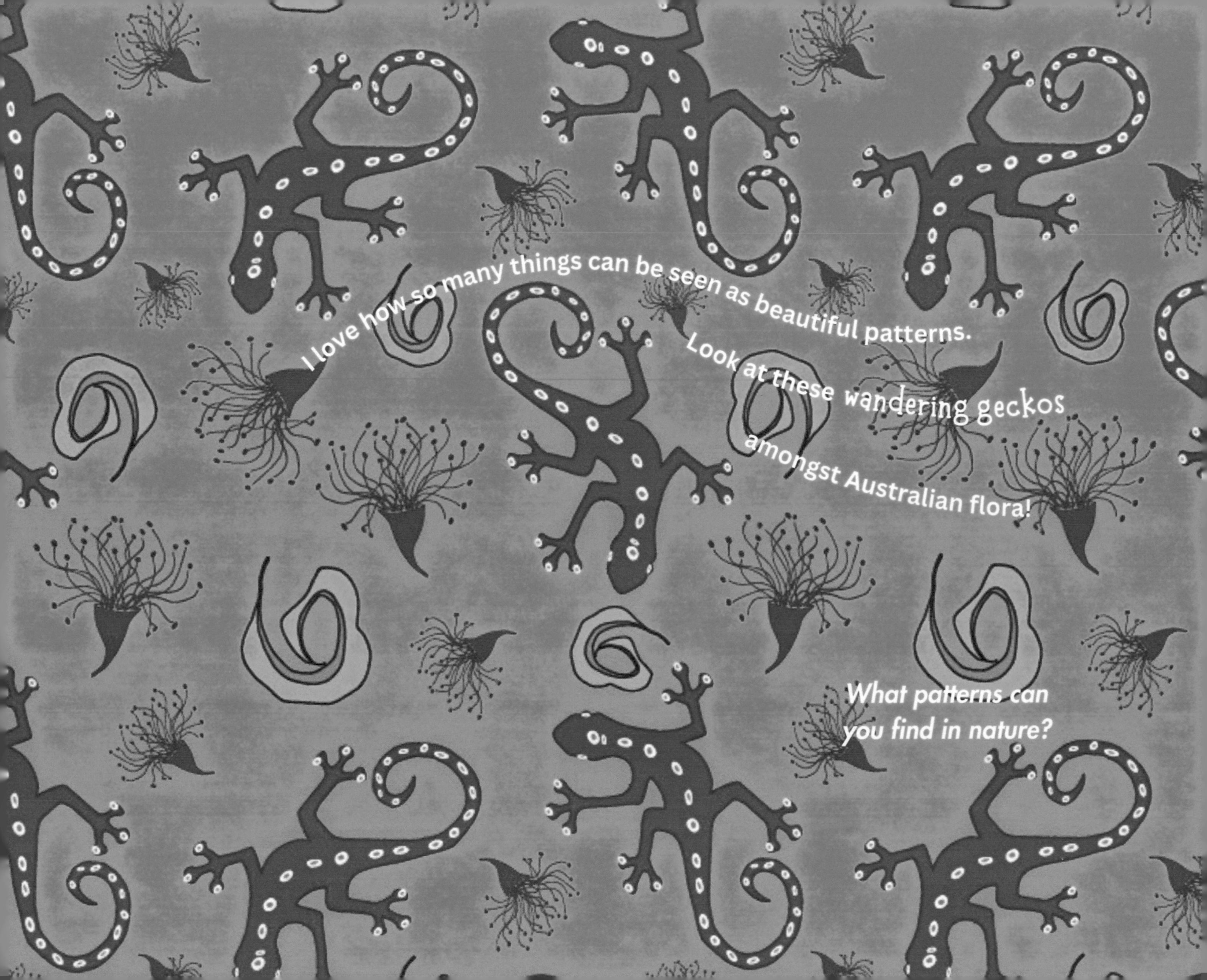

I love how so many things can be seen as beautiful patterns.
Look at these wandering geckos amongst Australian flora!
What patterns can you find in nature?

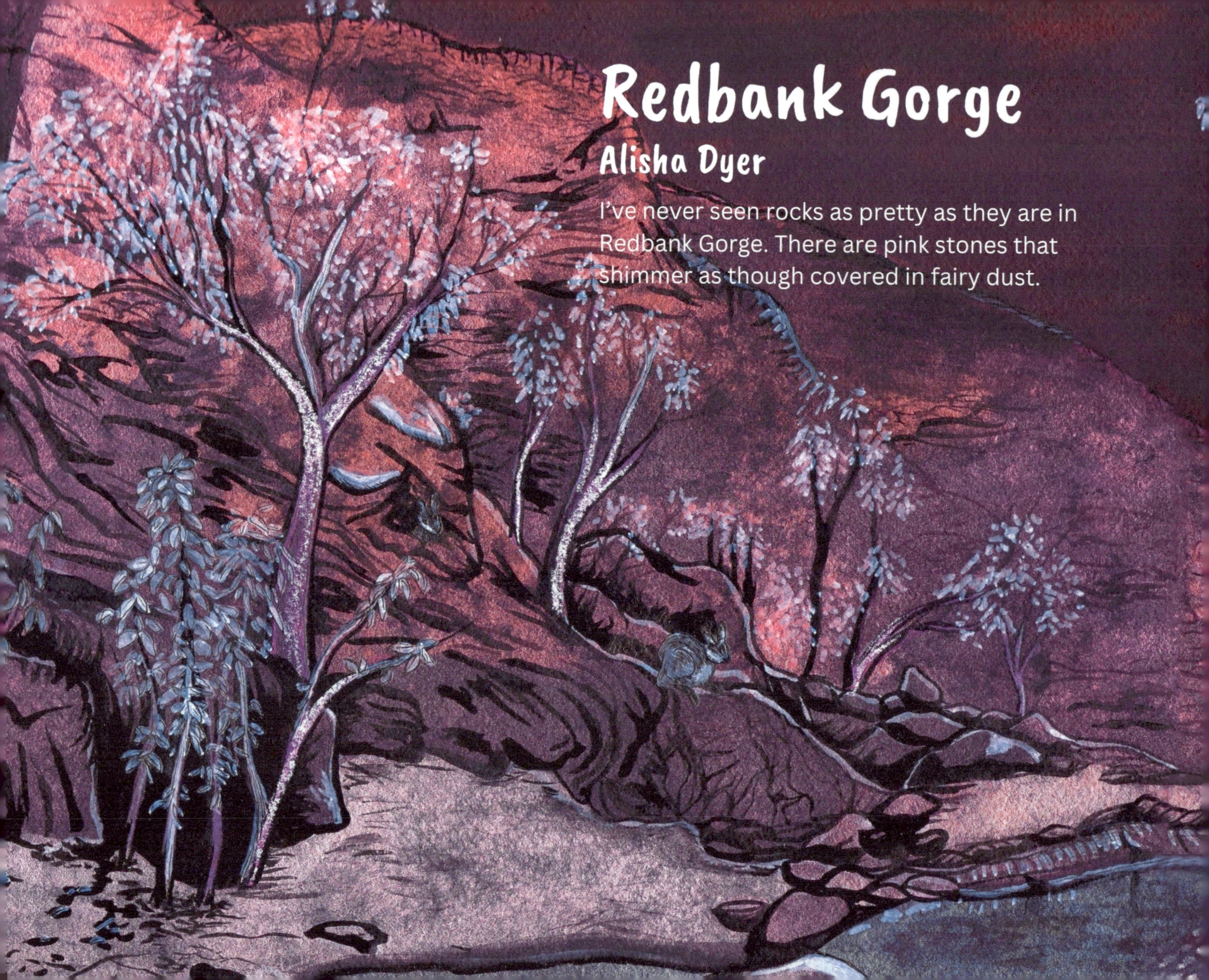

Redbank Gorge

Alisha Dyer

I've never seen rocks as pretty as they are in Redbank Gorge. There are pink stones that shimmer as though covered in fairy dust.

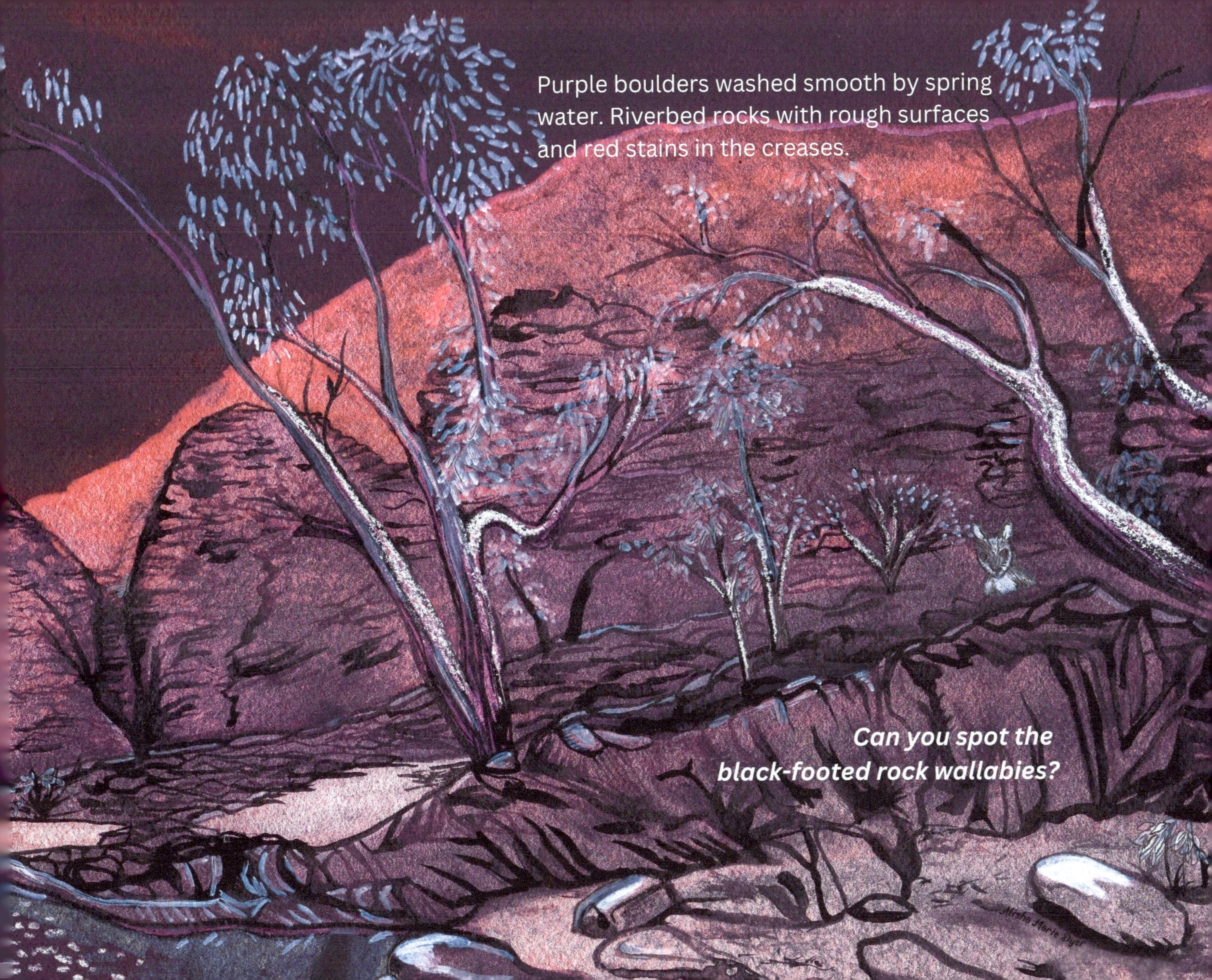

Purple boulders washed smooth by spring water. Riverbed rocks with rough surfaces and red stains in the creases.

Can you spot the black-footed rock wallabies?

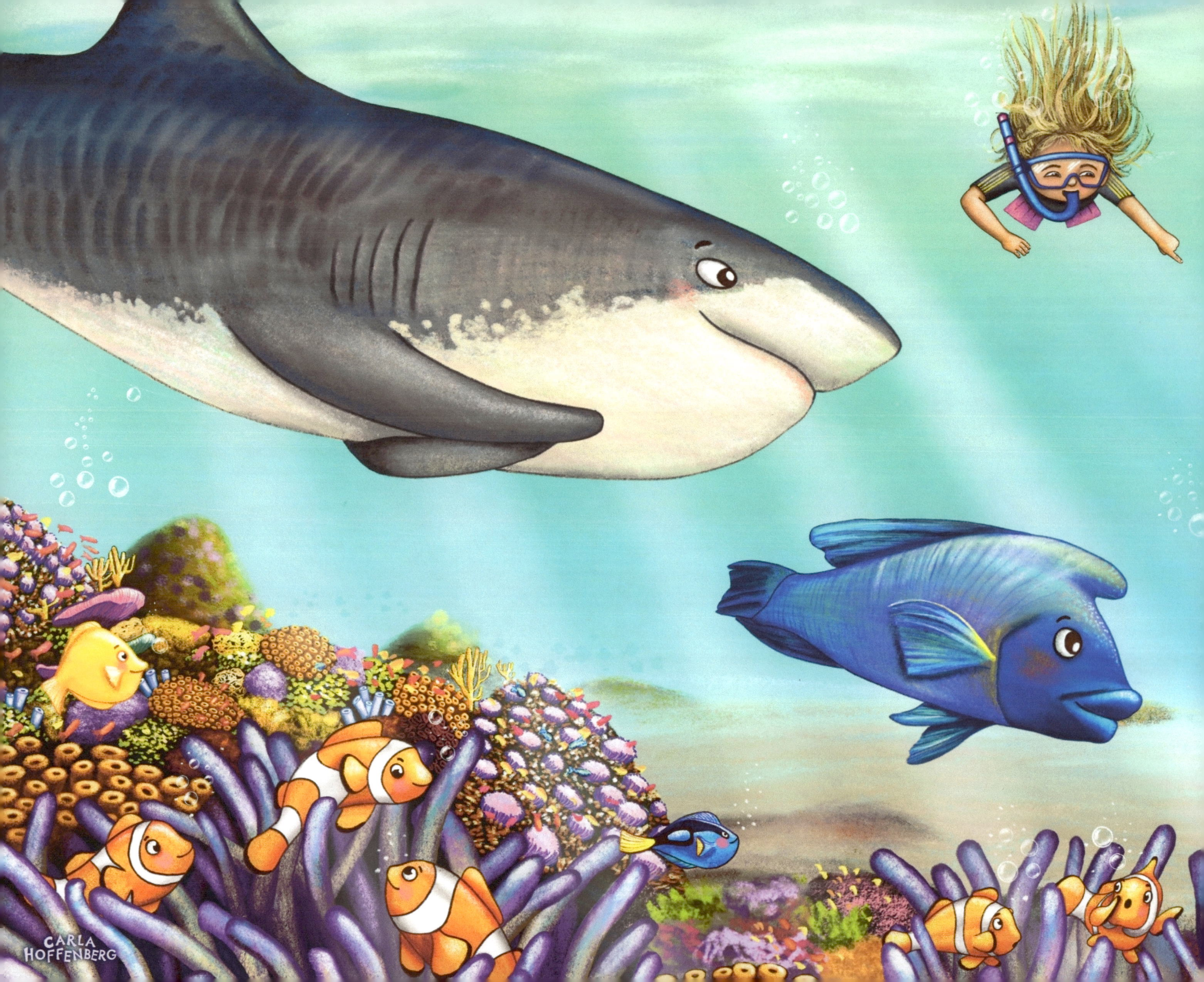

CARLA
HOFFENBERG

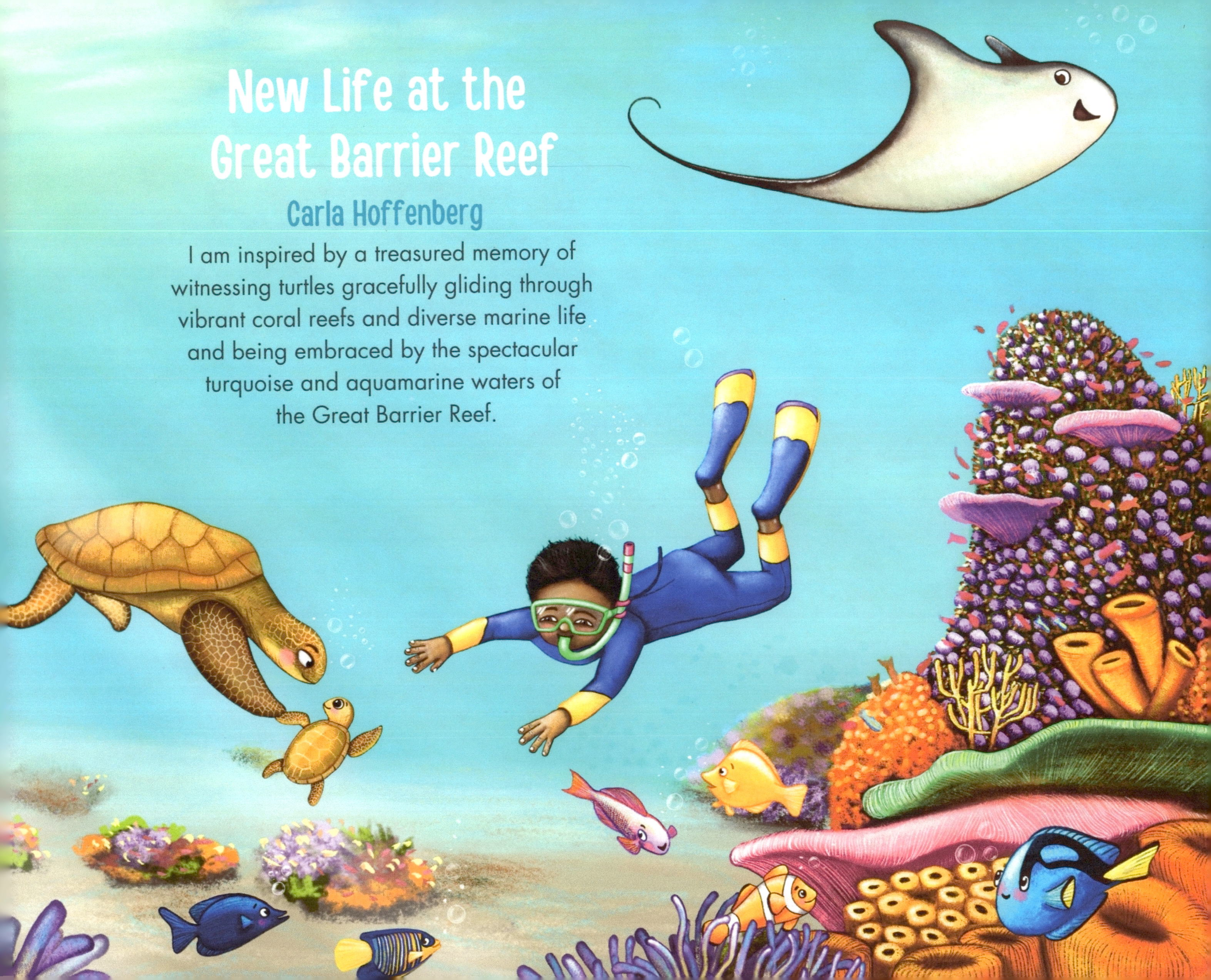

New Life at the
Great Barrier Reef
Carla Hoffenberg
I am inspired by a treasured memory of
witnessing turtles gracefully gliding through
vibrant coral reefs and diverse marine life
and being embraced by the spectacular
turquoise and aquamarine waters of
the Great Barrier Reef.

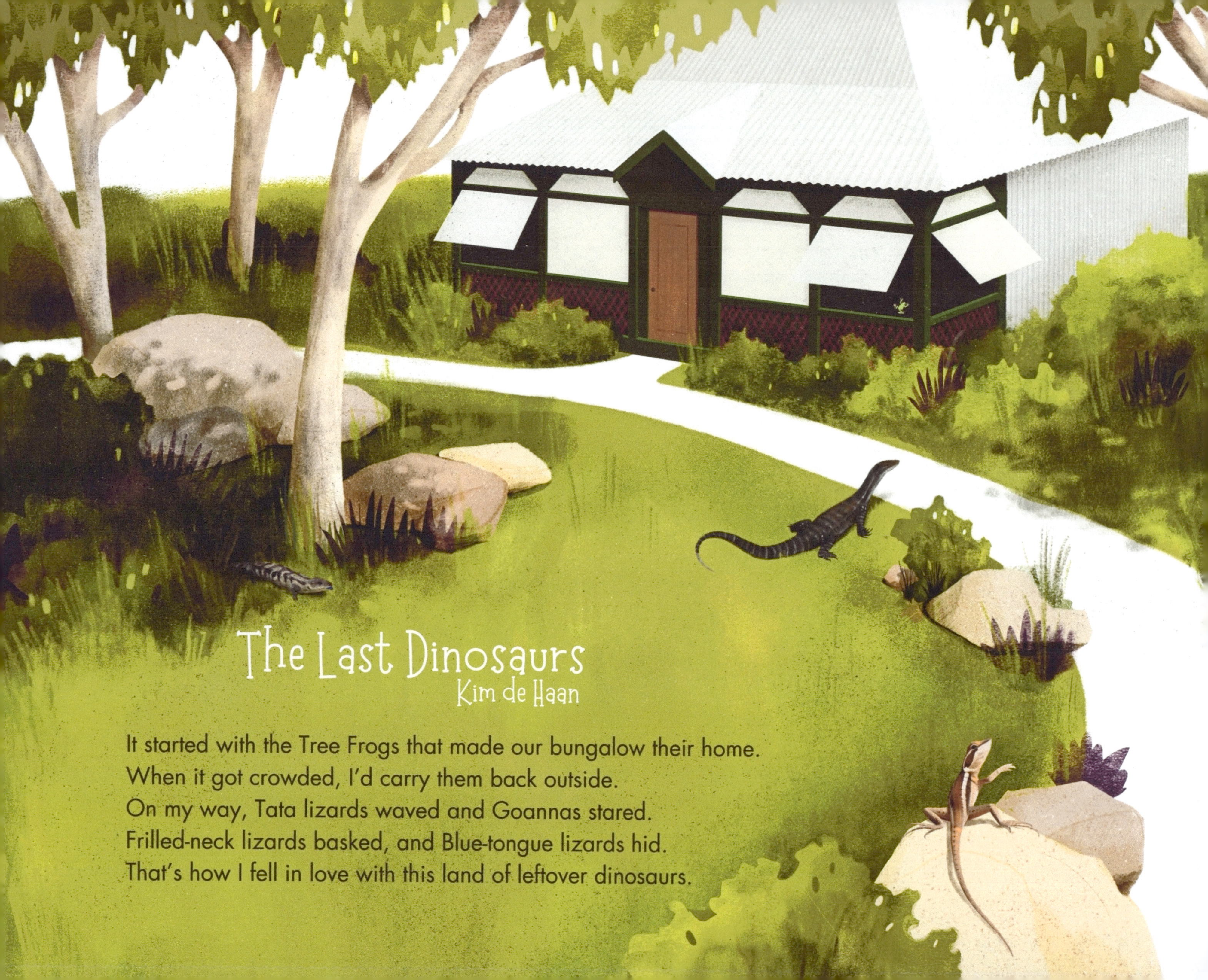

The Last Dinosaurs
Kim de Haan

It started with the Tree Frogs that made our bungalow their home.
When it got crowded, I'd carry them back outside.
On my way, Tata lizards waved and Goannas stared.
Frilled-neck lizards basked, and Blue-tongue lizards hid.
That's how I fell in love with this land of leftover dinosaurs.

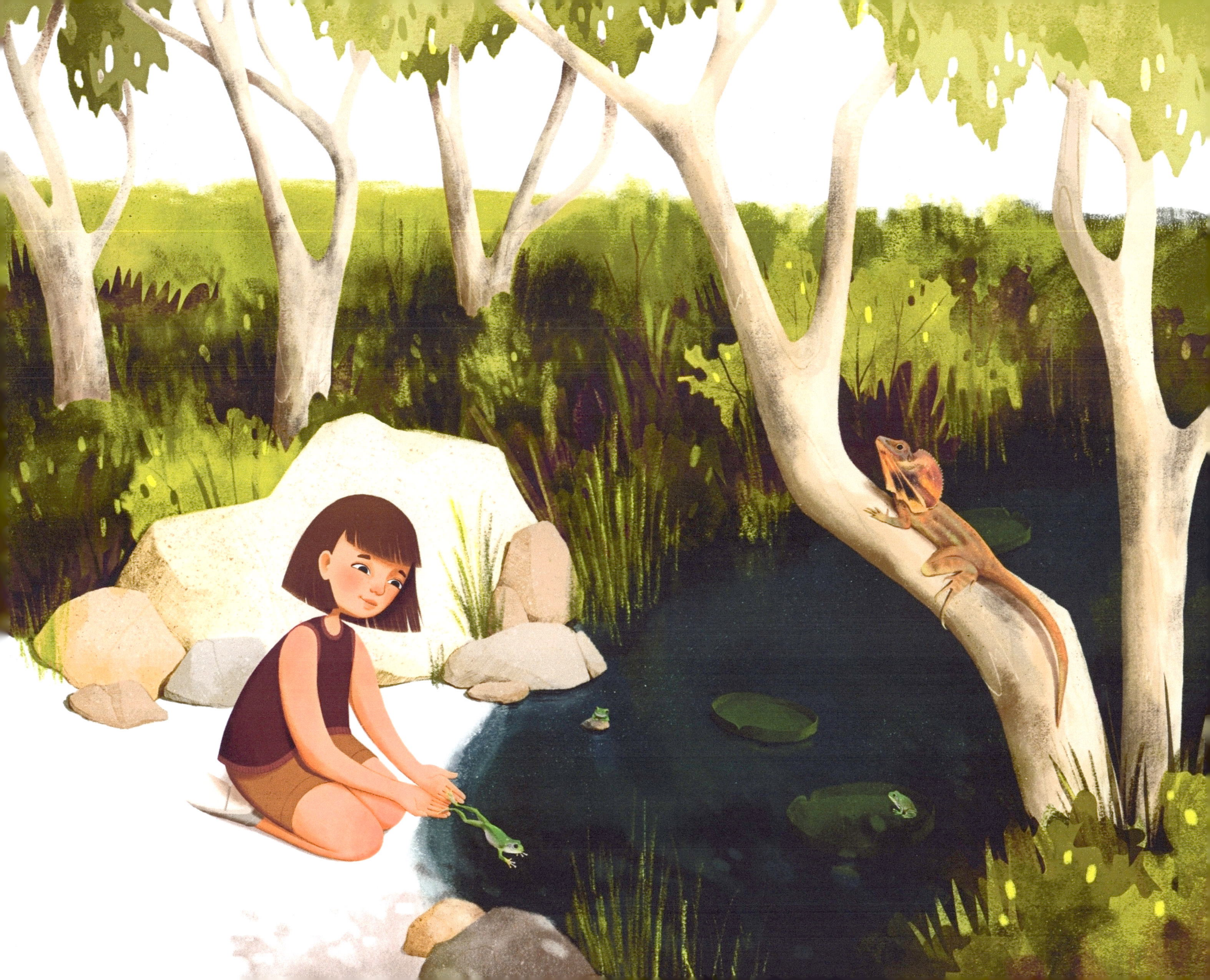

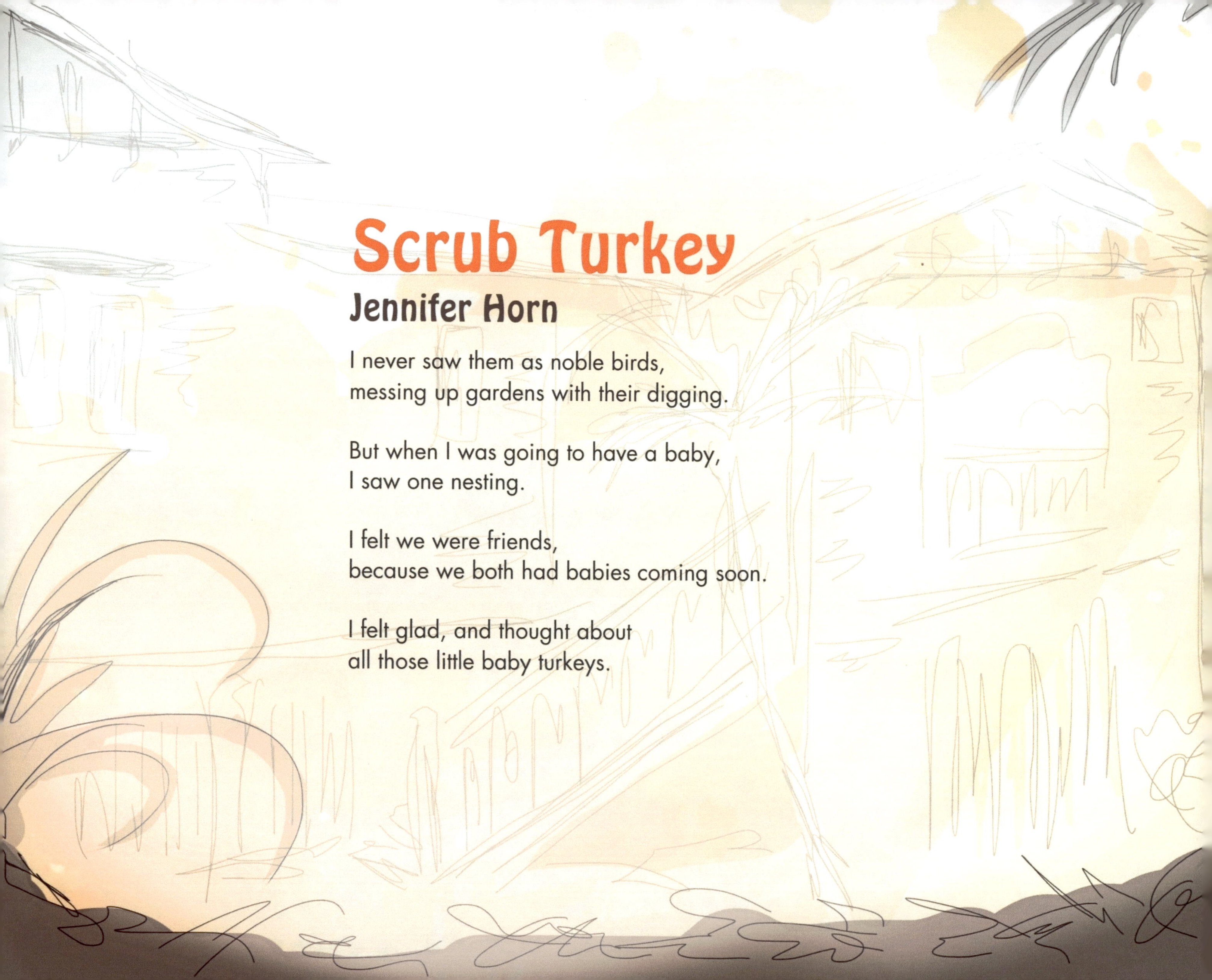

Scrub Turkey

Jennifer Horn

I never saw them as noble birds,
messing up gardens with their digging.

But when I was going to have a baby,
I saw one nesting.

I felt we were friends,
because we both had babies coming soon.

I felt glad, and thought about
all those little baby turkeys.

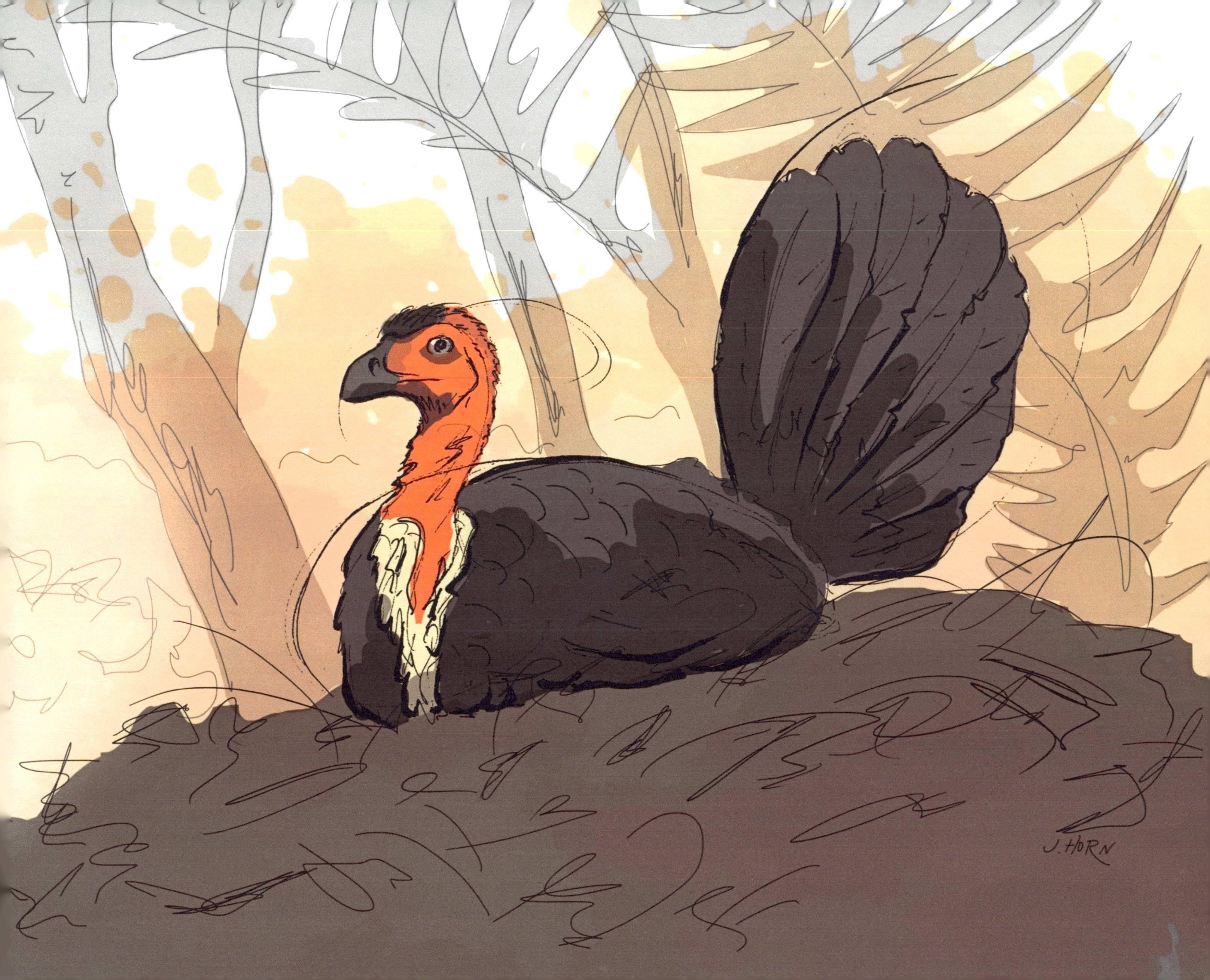
J. Horn

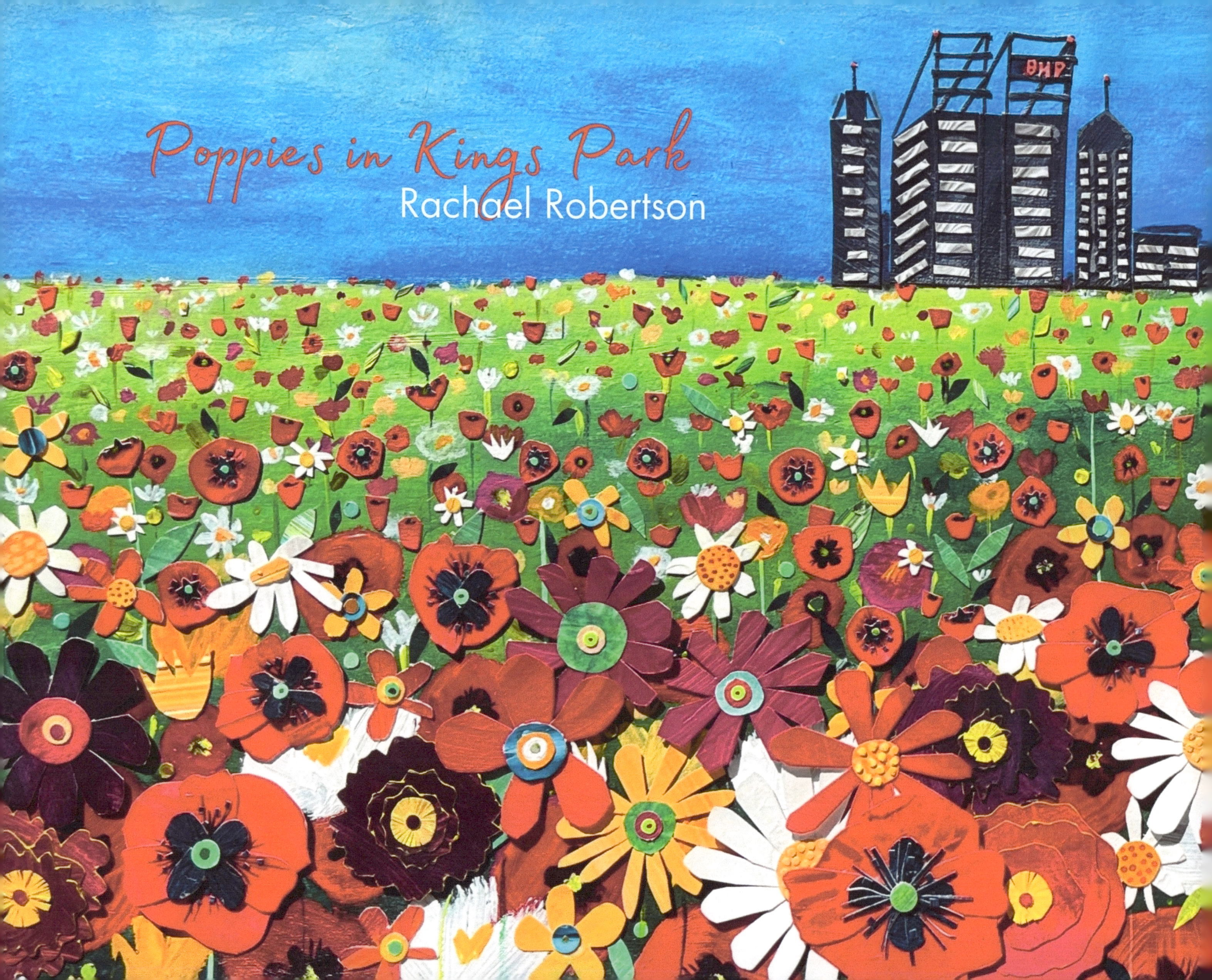
Poppies in Kings Park
Rachael Robertson

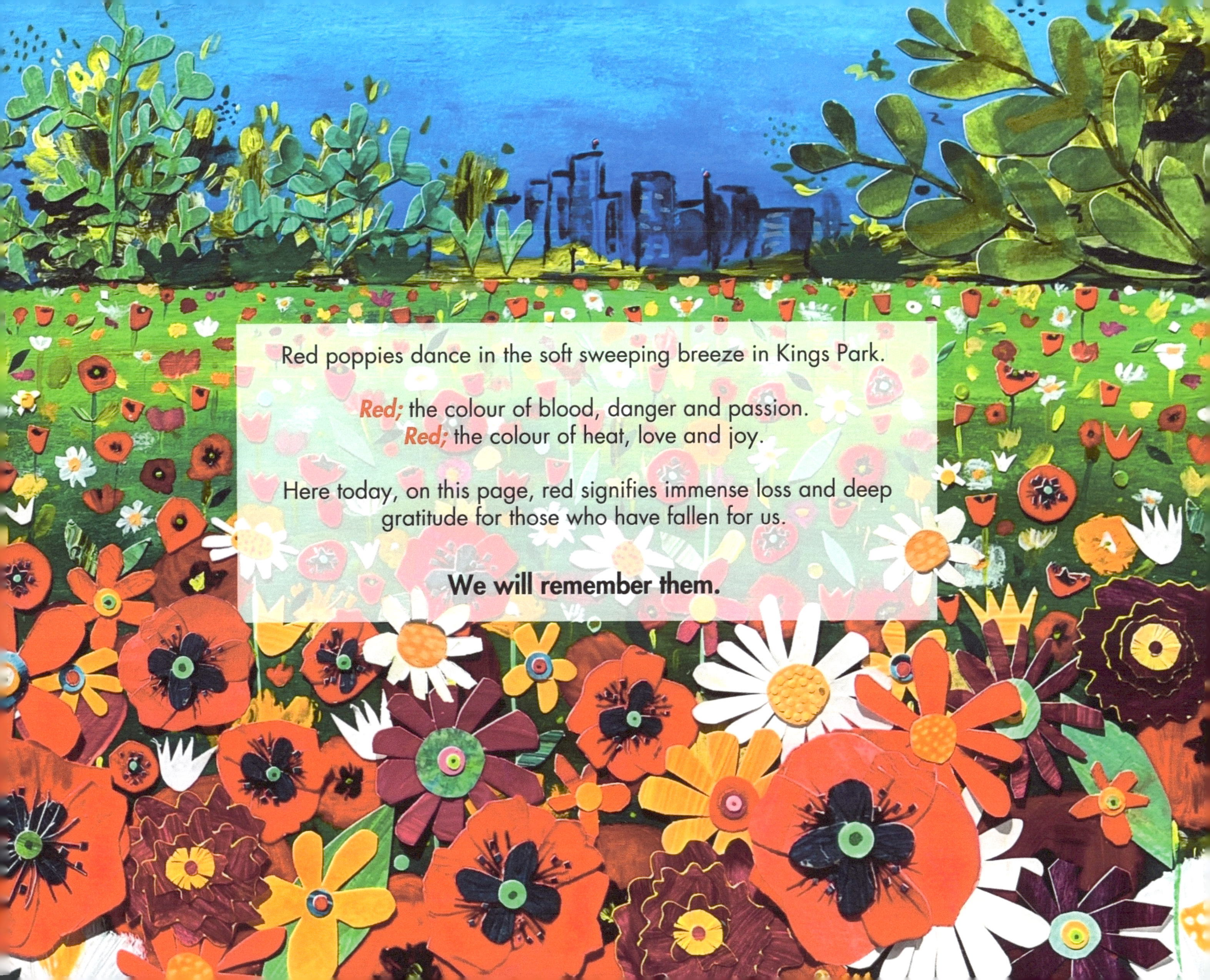

Red poppies dance in the soft sweeping breeze in Kings Park.

Red; the colour of blood, danger and passion.
Red; the colour of heat, love and joy.

Here today, on this page, red signifies immense loss and deep gratitude for those who have fallen for us.

We will remember them.

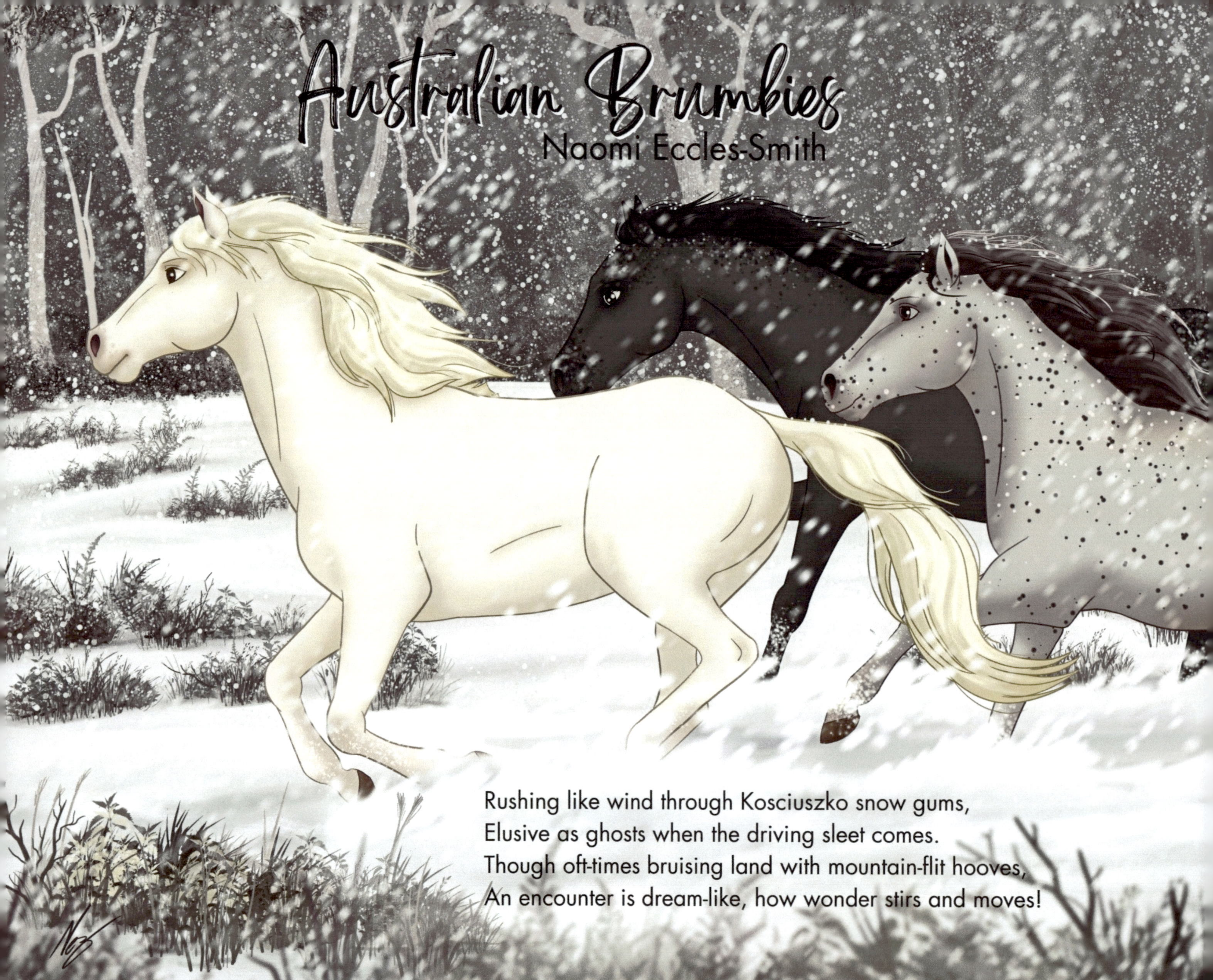

Australian Brumbies
Naomi Eccles-Smith

Rushing like wind through Kosciuszko snow gums,
Elusive as ghosts when the driving sleet comes.
Though oft-times bruising land with mountain-flit hooves,
An encounter is dream-like, how wonder stirs and moves!

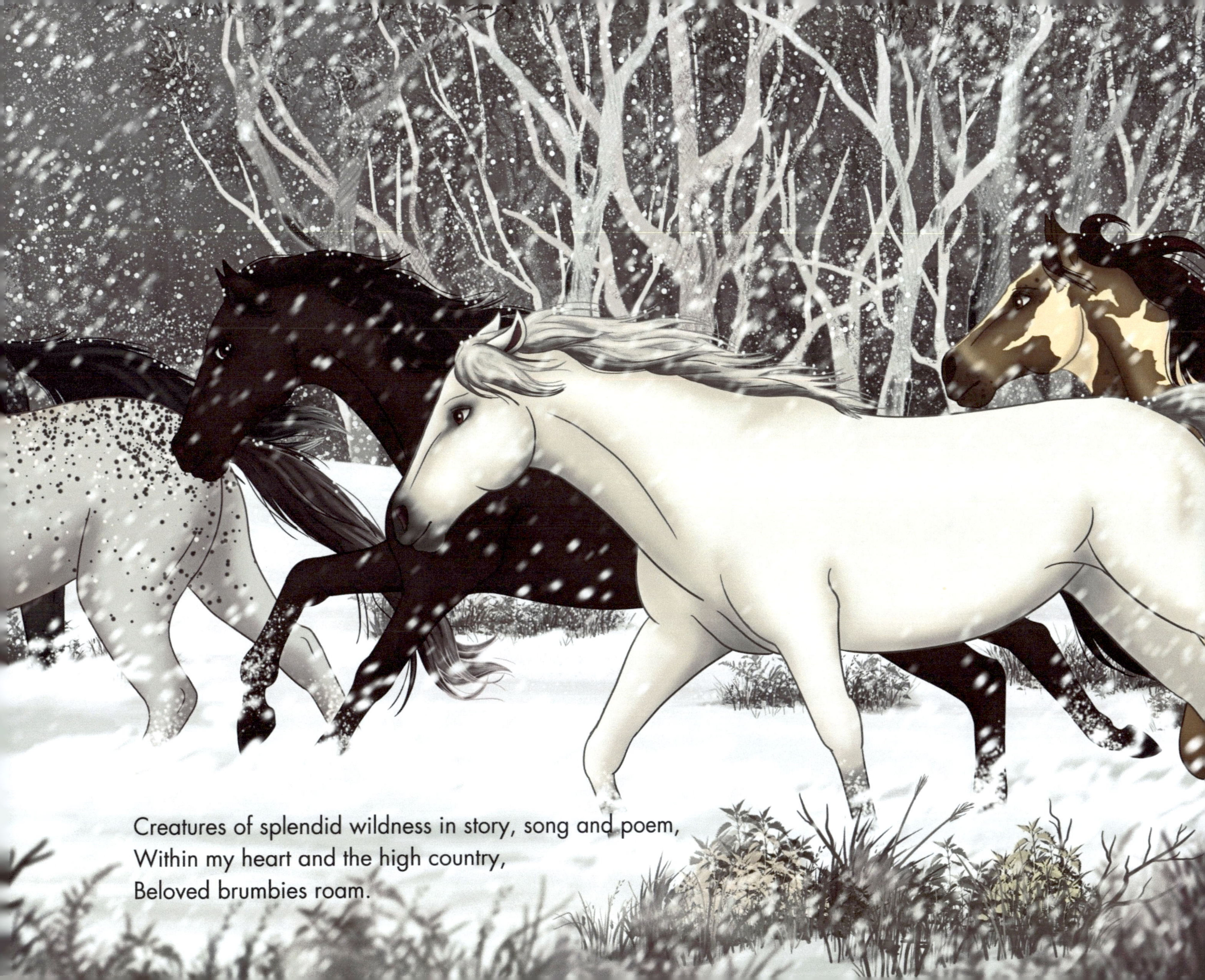

Creatures of splendid wildness in story, song and poem,
Within my heart and the high country,
Beloved brumbies roam.

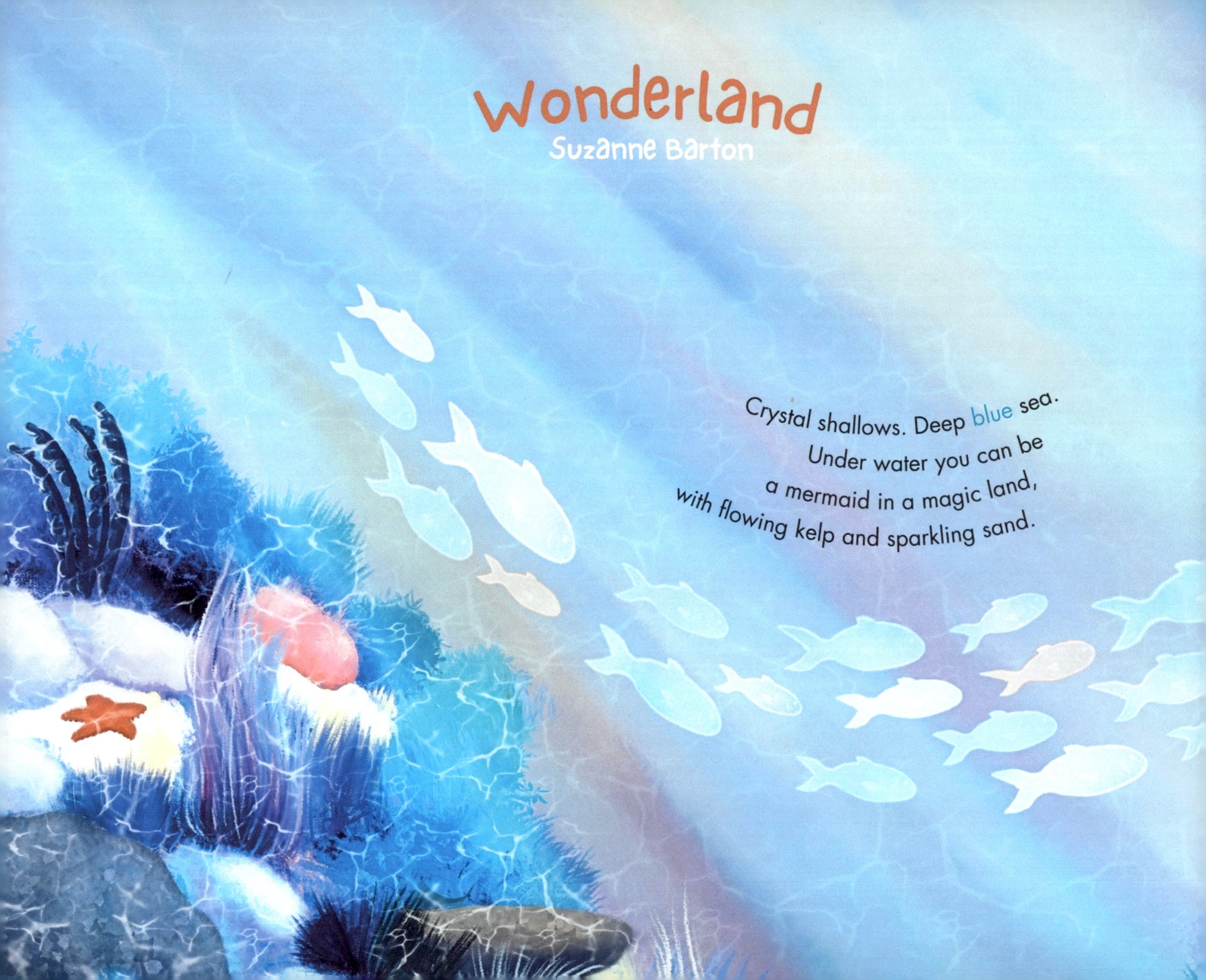

Wonderland
Suzanne Barton

Crystal shallows. Deep blue sea.
Under water you can be
a mermaid in a magic land,
with flowing kelp and sparkling sand.

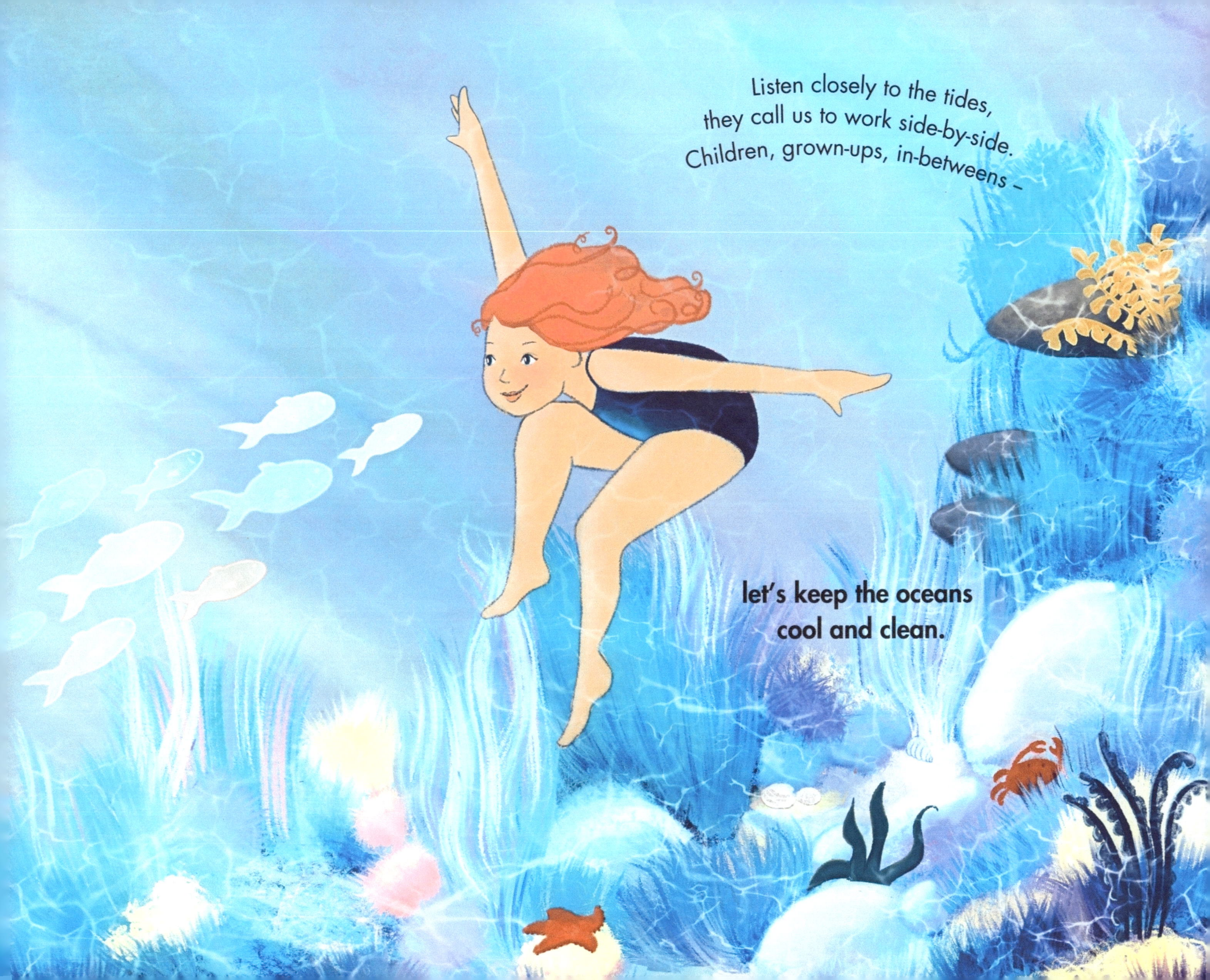

Listen closely to the tides,
they call us to work side-by-side.
Children, grown-ups, in-betweens –

let's keep the oceans
cool and clean.

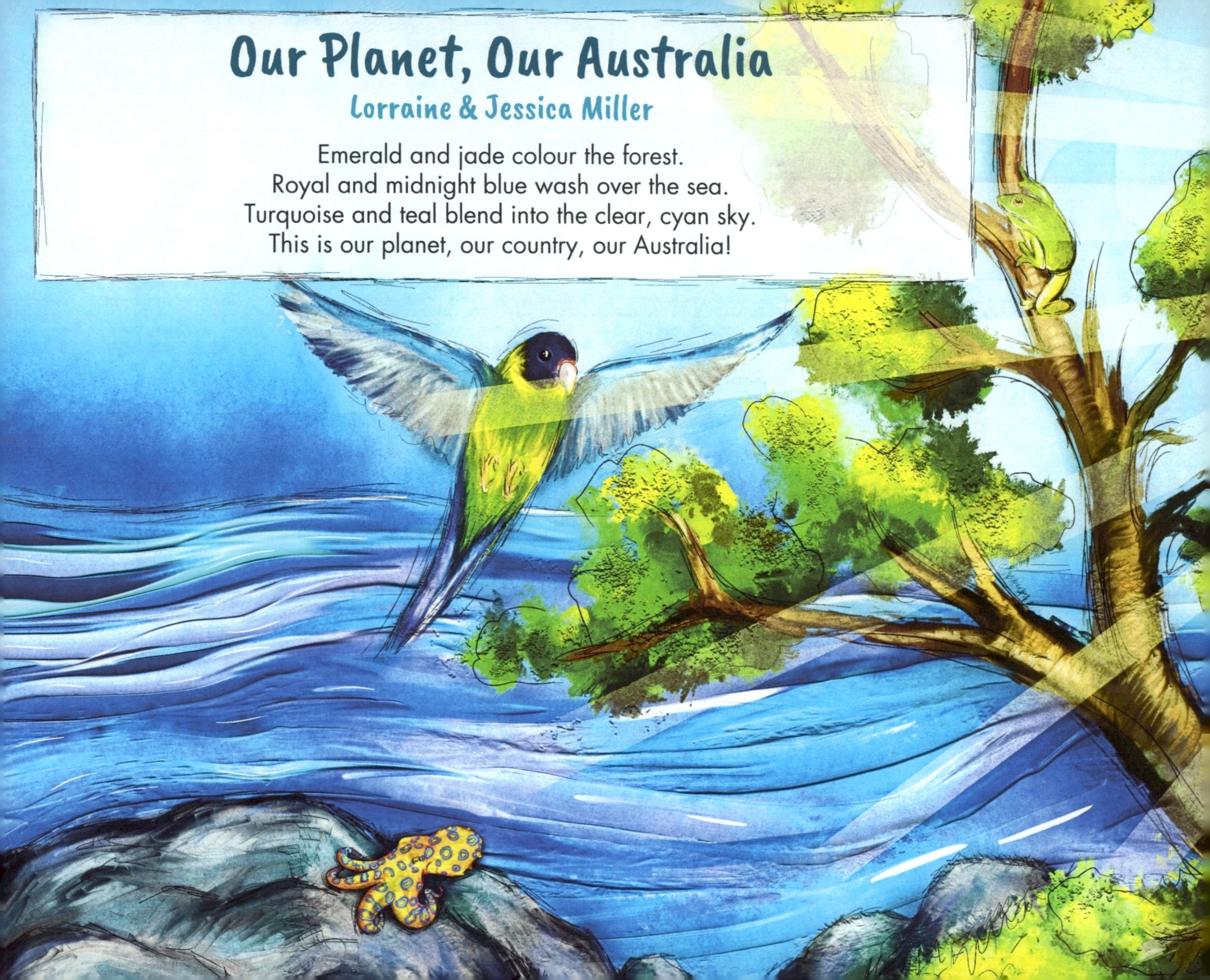

Our Planet, Our Australia

Lorraine & Jessica Miller

Emerald and jade colour the forest.
Royal and midnight blue wash over the sea.
Turquoise and teal blend into the clear, cyan sky.
This is our planet, our country, our Australia!

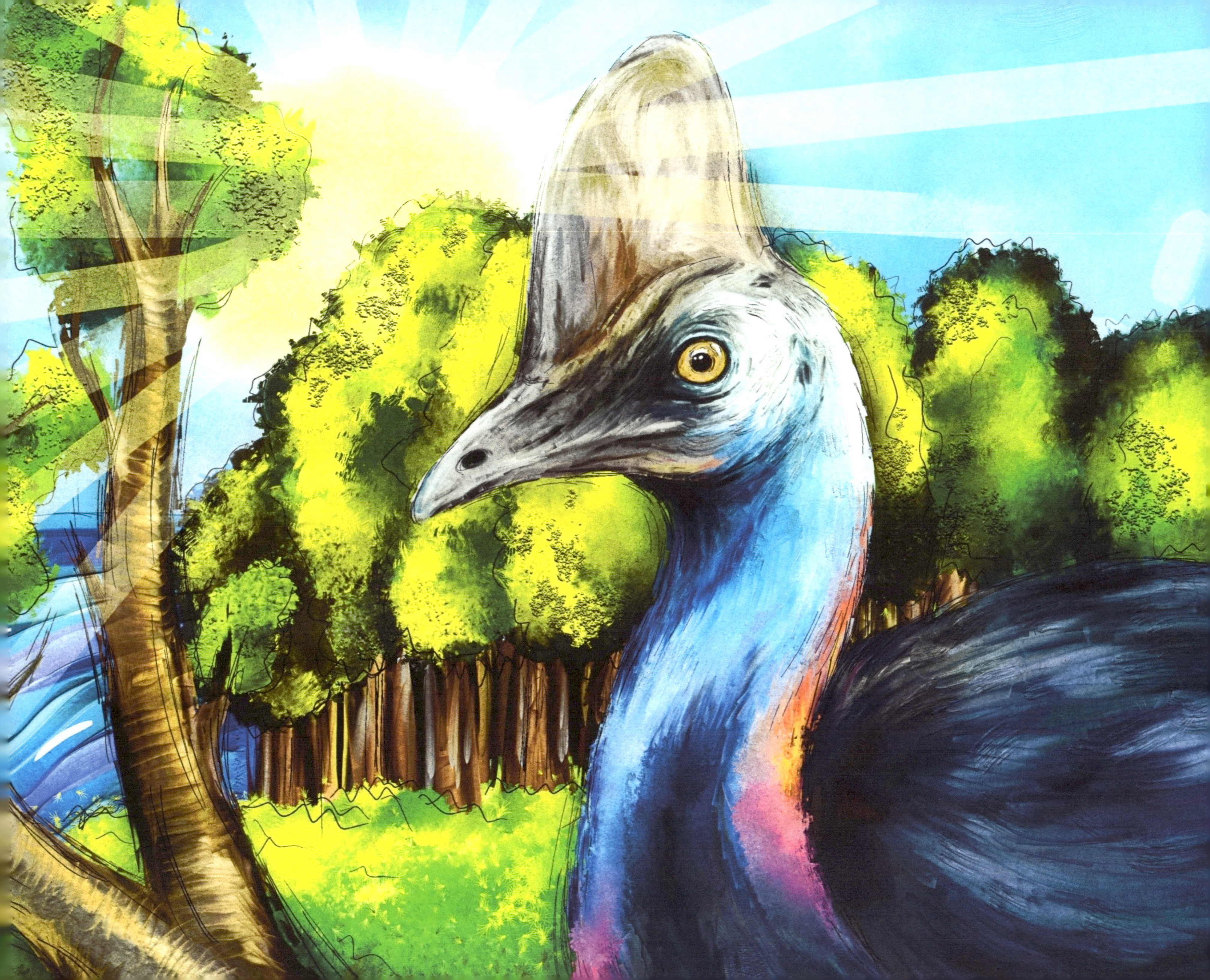

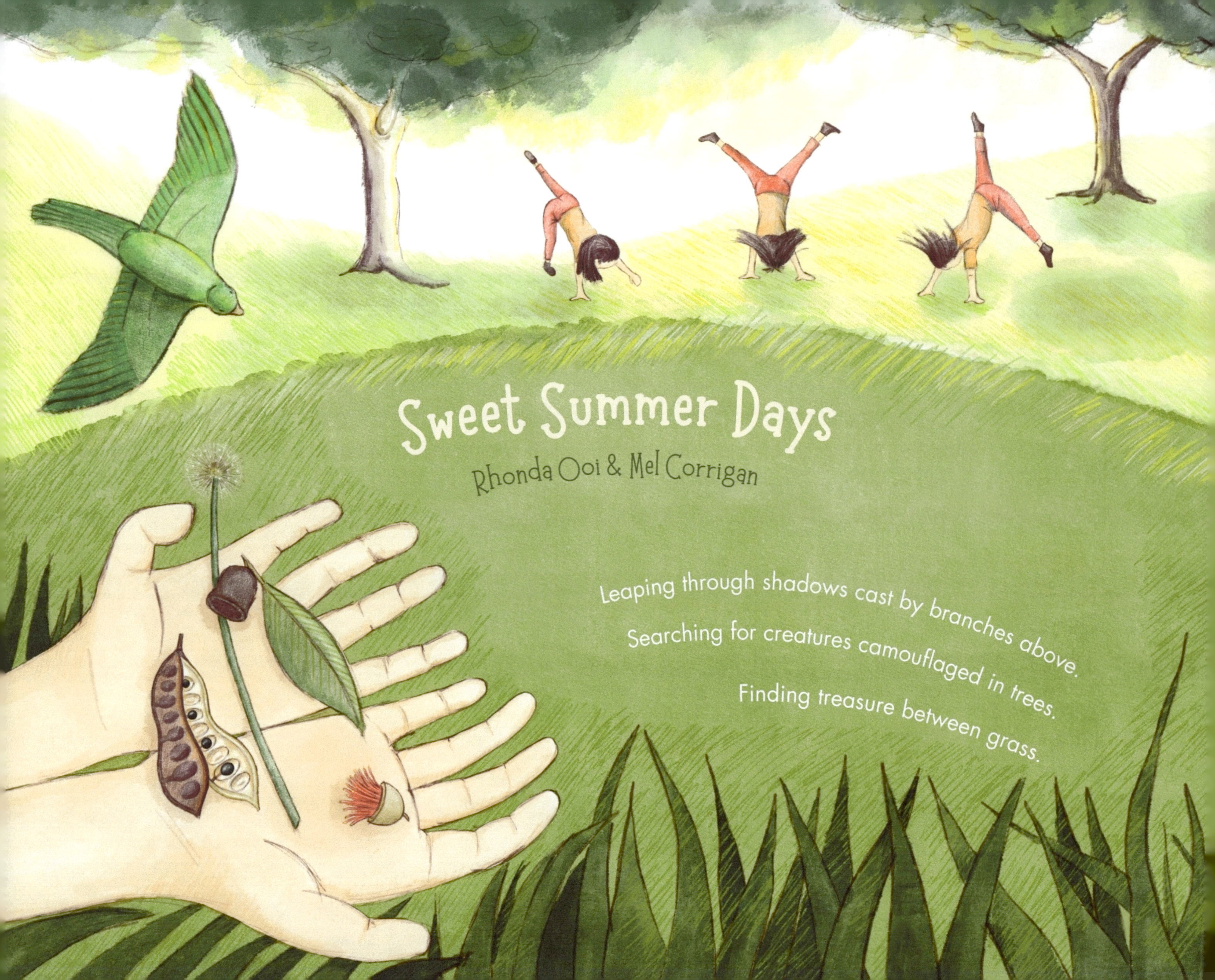

Sweet Summer Days
Rhonda Ooi & Mel Corrigan
Leaping through shadows cast by branches above.
Searching for creatures camouflaged in trees.
Finding treasure between grass.

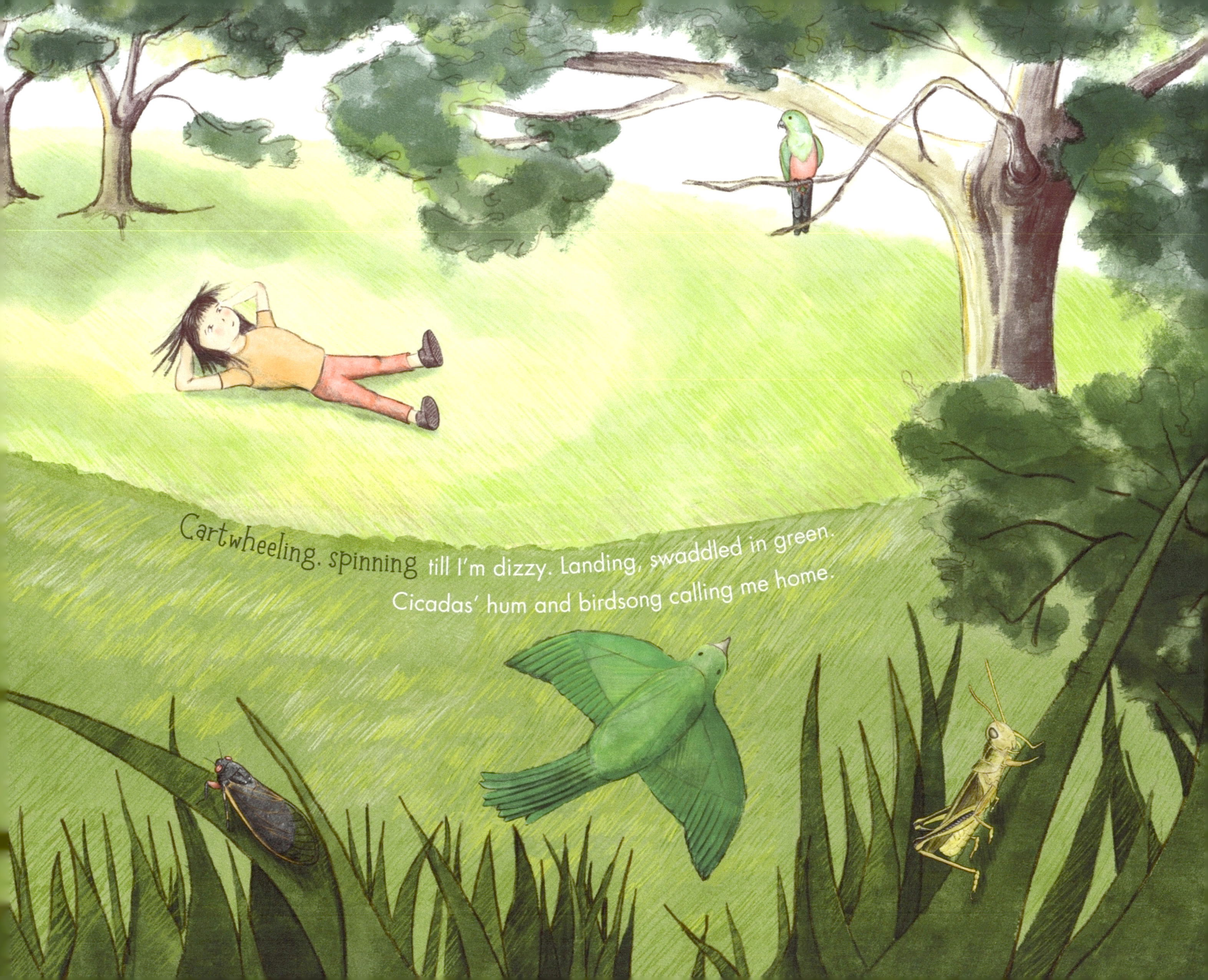
Cartwheeling, spinning till I'm dizzy. Landing, swaddled in green.
Cicadas' hum and birdsong calling me home.

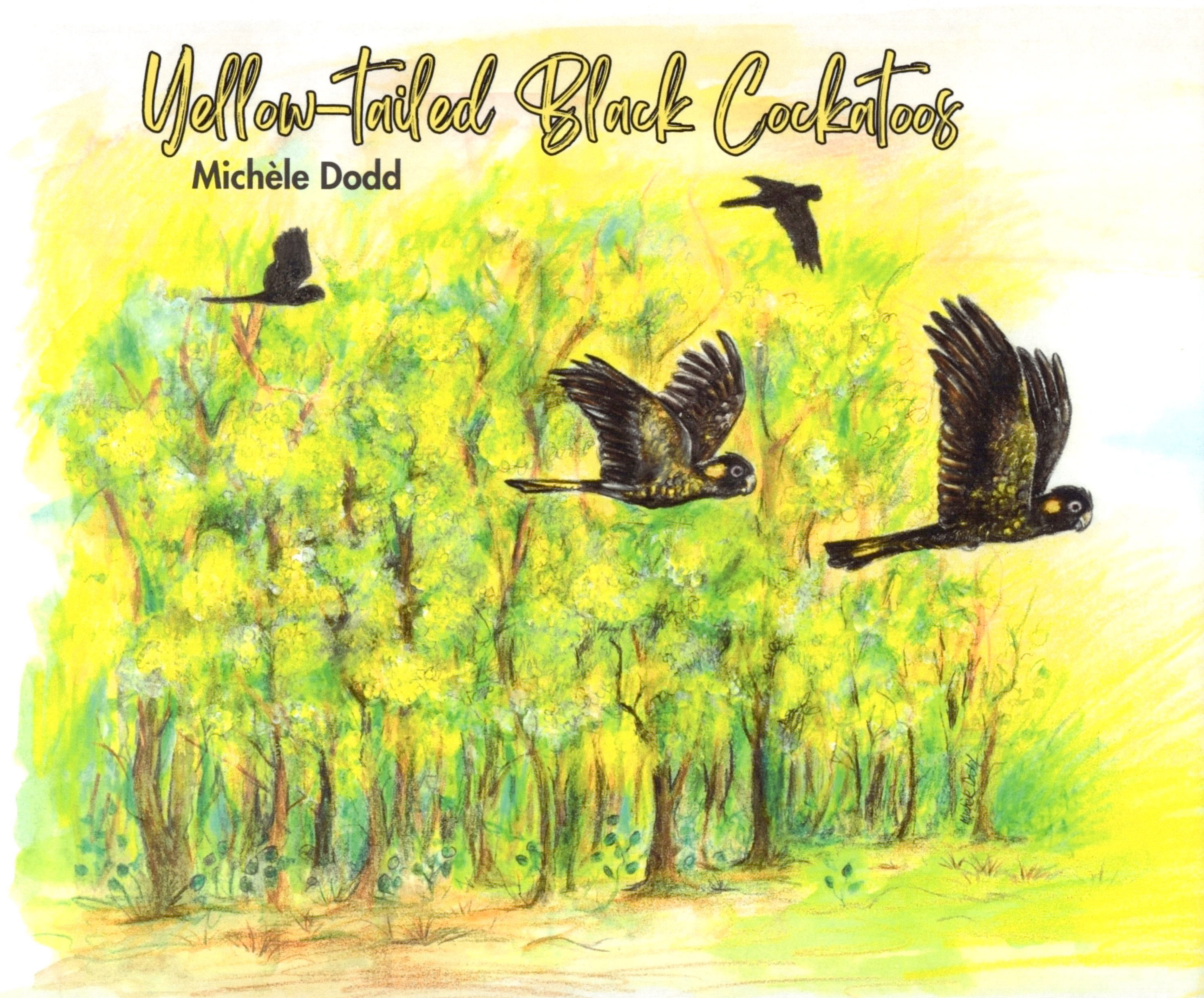

Yellow-tailed Black Cockatoos
Michèle Dodd

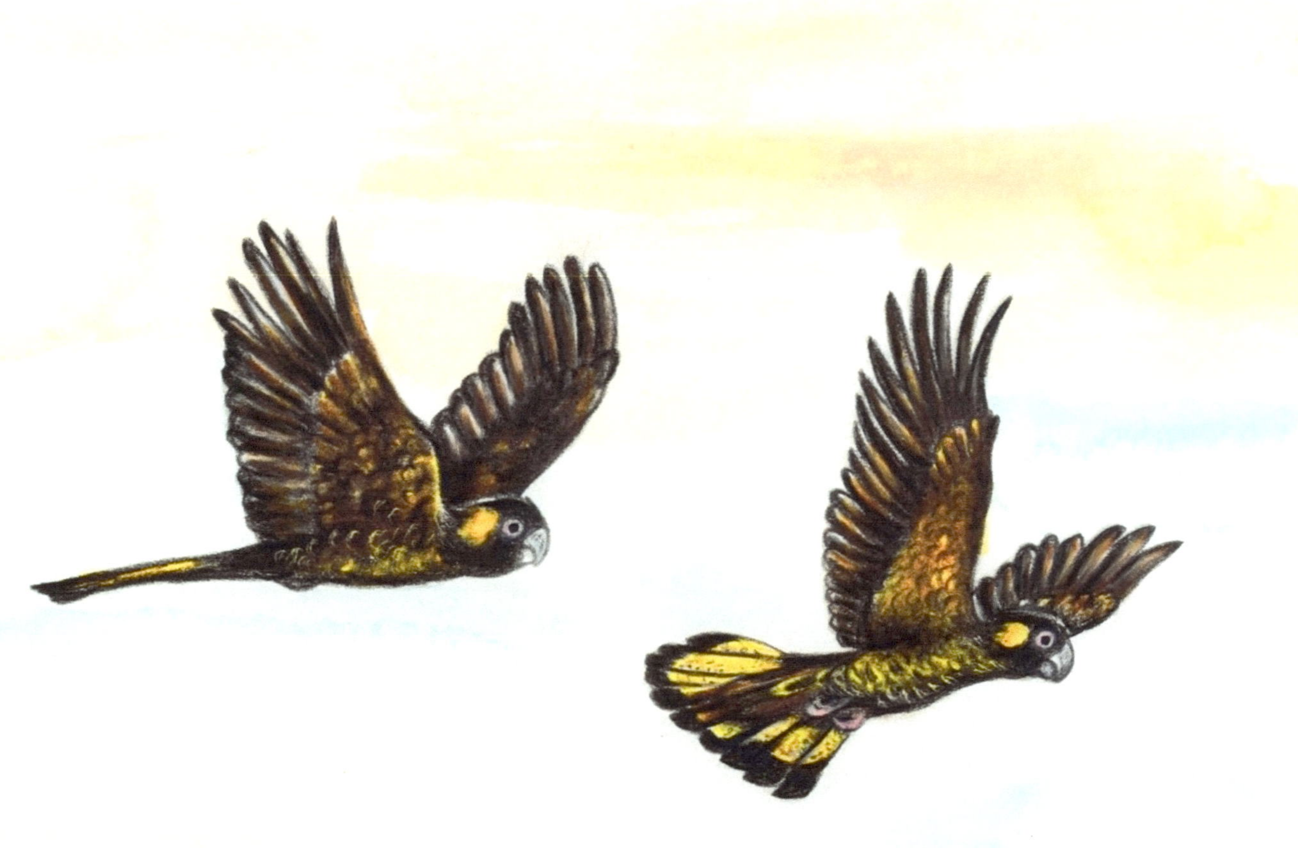

Sprinkles of golden wattle add splashes of sunshine to the Australian bush during August.

Haunting wails sound out as a flock of Yellow-tailed Black Cockatoos cruise in slow motion across the sky.

Such a magical time and place.

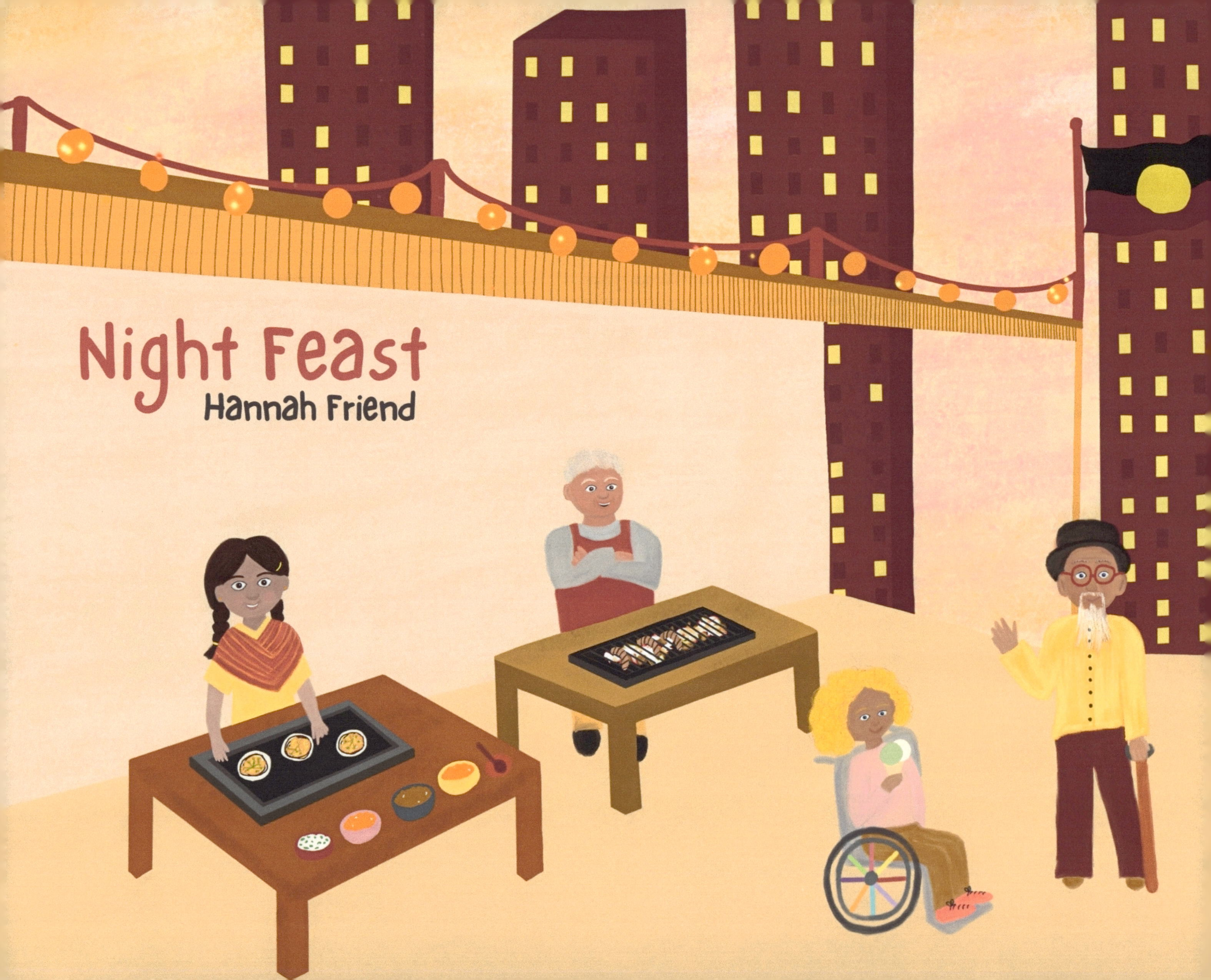

Night Feast
Hannah Friend

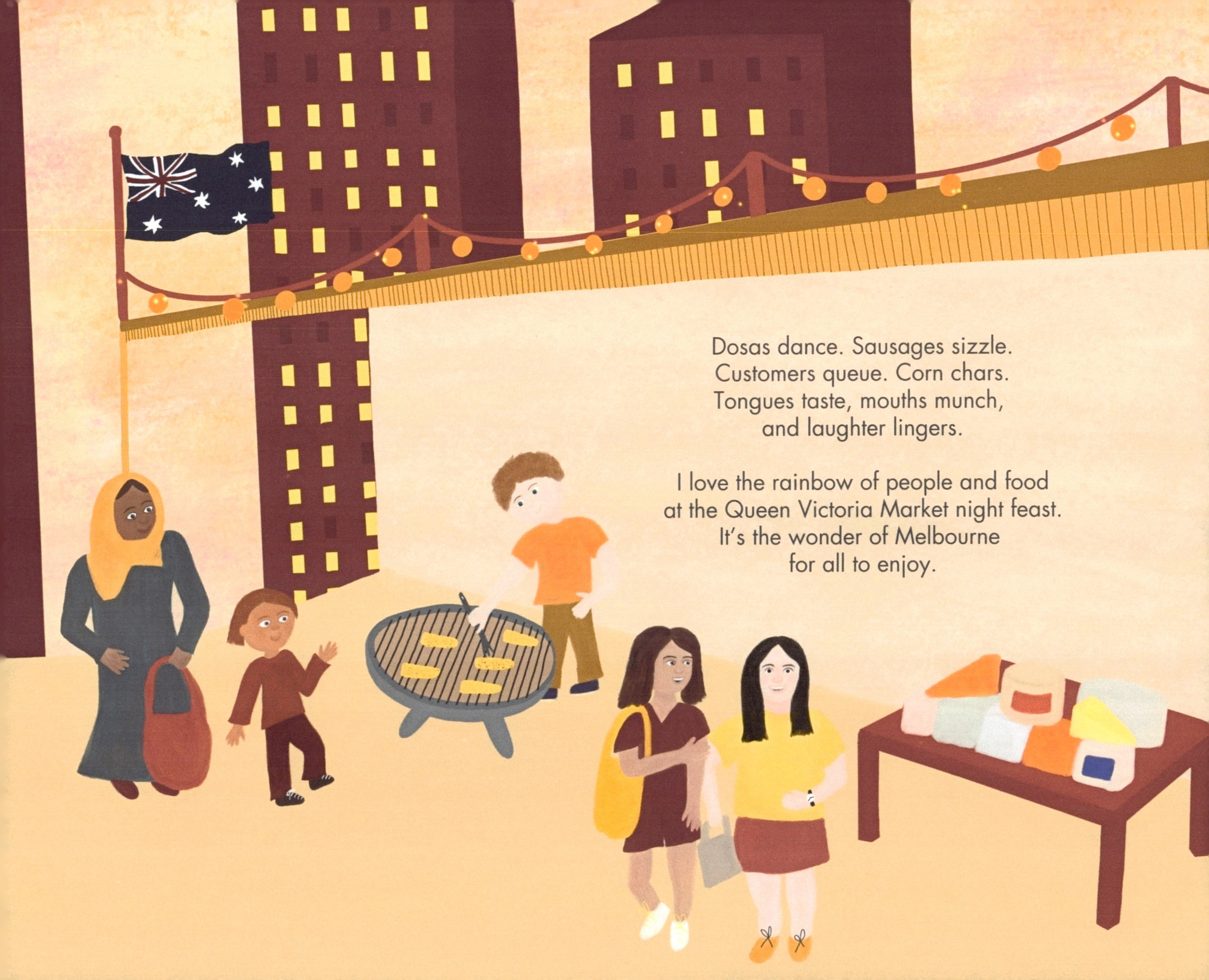

Dosas dance. Sausages sizzle.
Customers queue. Corn chars.
Tongues taste, mouths munch,
and laughter lingers.

I love the rainbow of people and food
at the Queen Victoria Market night feast.
It's the wonder of Melbourne
for all to enjoy.

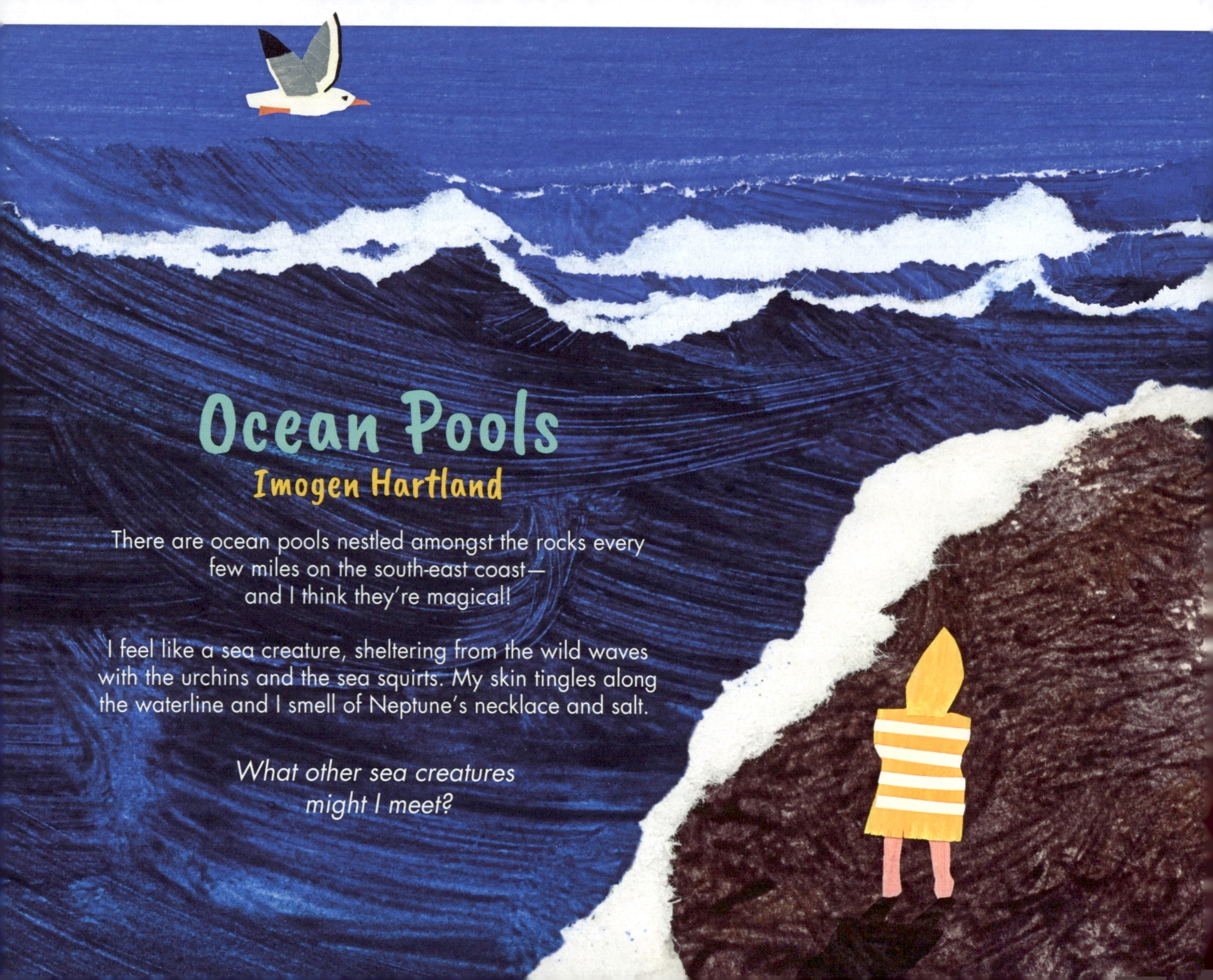

Ocean Pools
Imogen Hartland

There are ocean pools nestled amongst the rocks every
few miles on the south-east coast—
and I think they're magical!

I feel like a sea creature, sheltering from the wild waves
with the urchins and the sea squirts. My skin tingles along
the waterline and I smell of Neptune's necklace and salt.

*What other sea creatures
might I meet?*

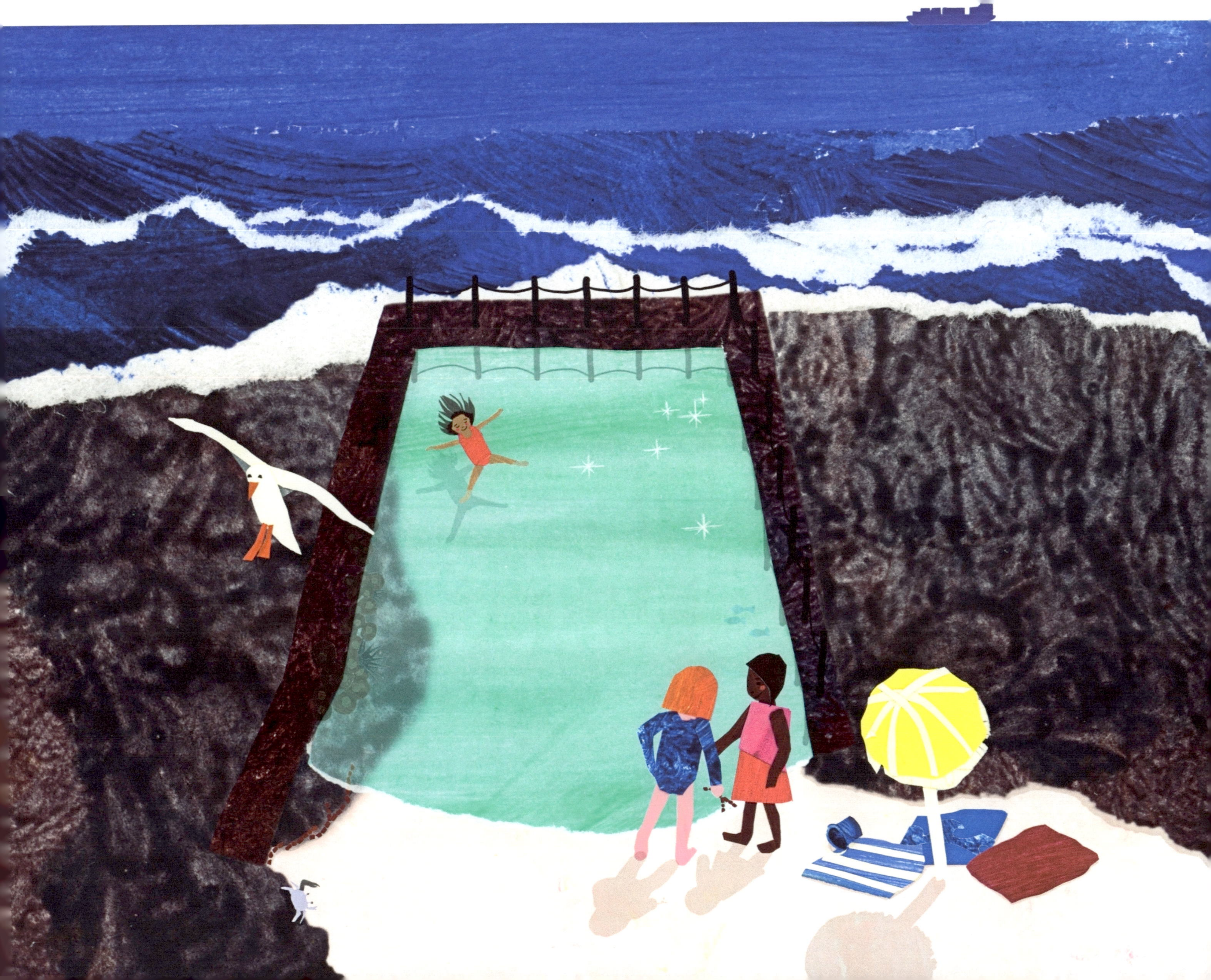

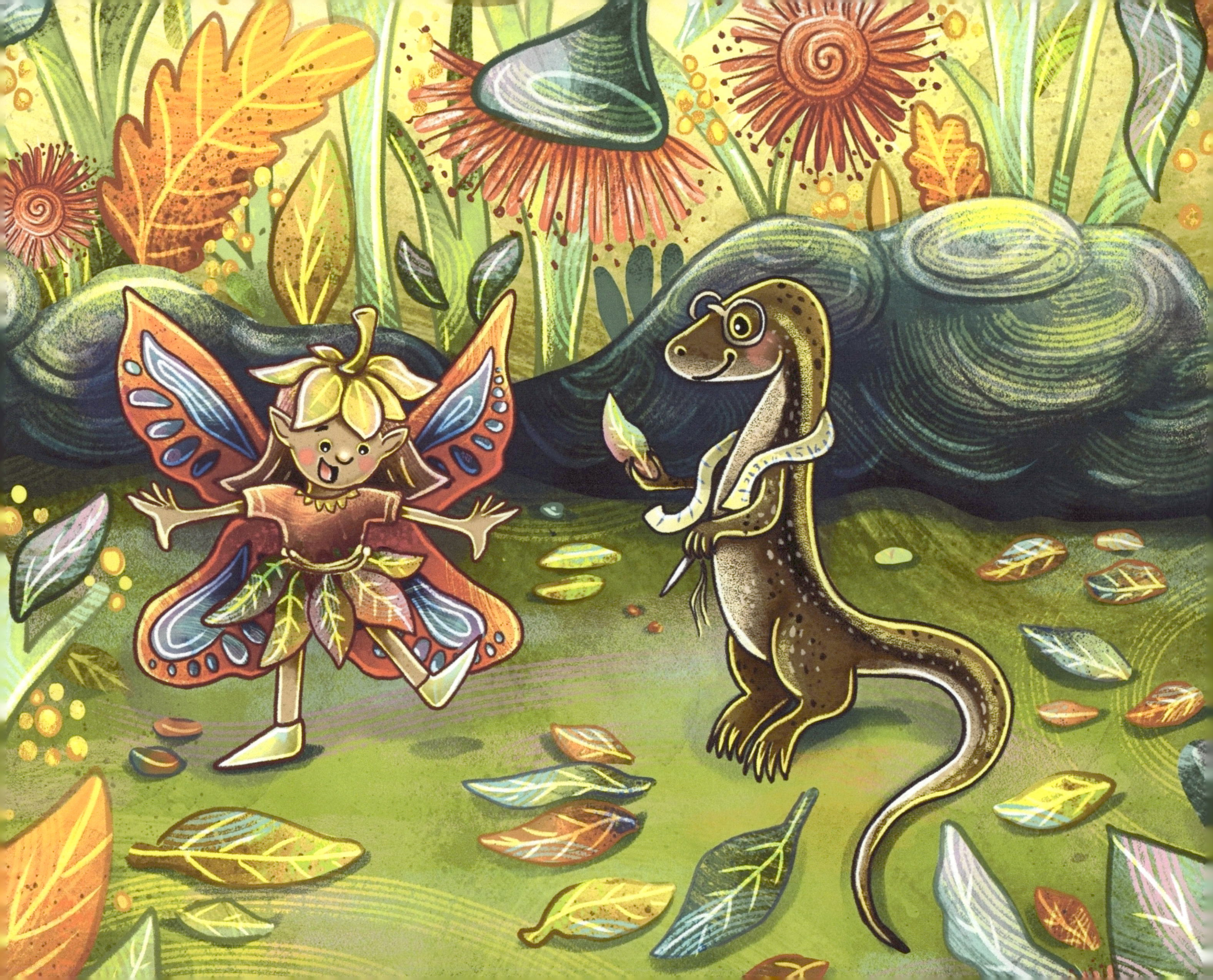

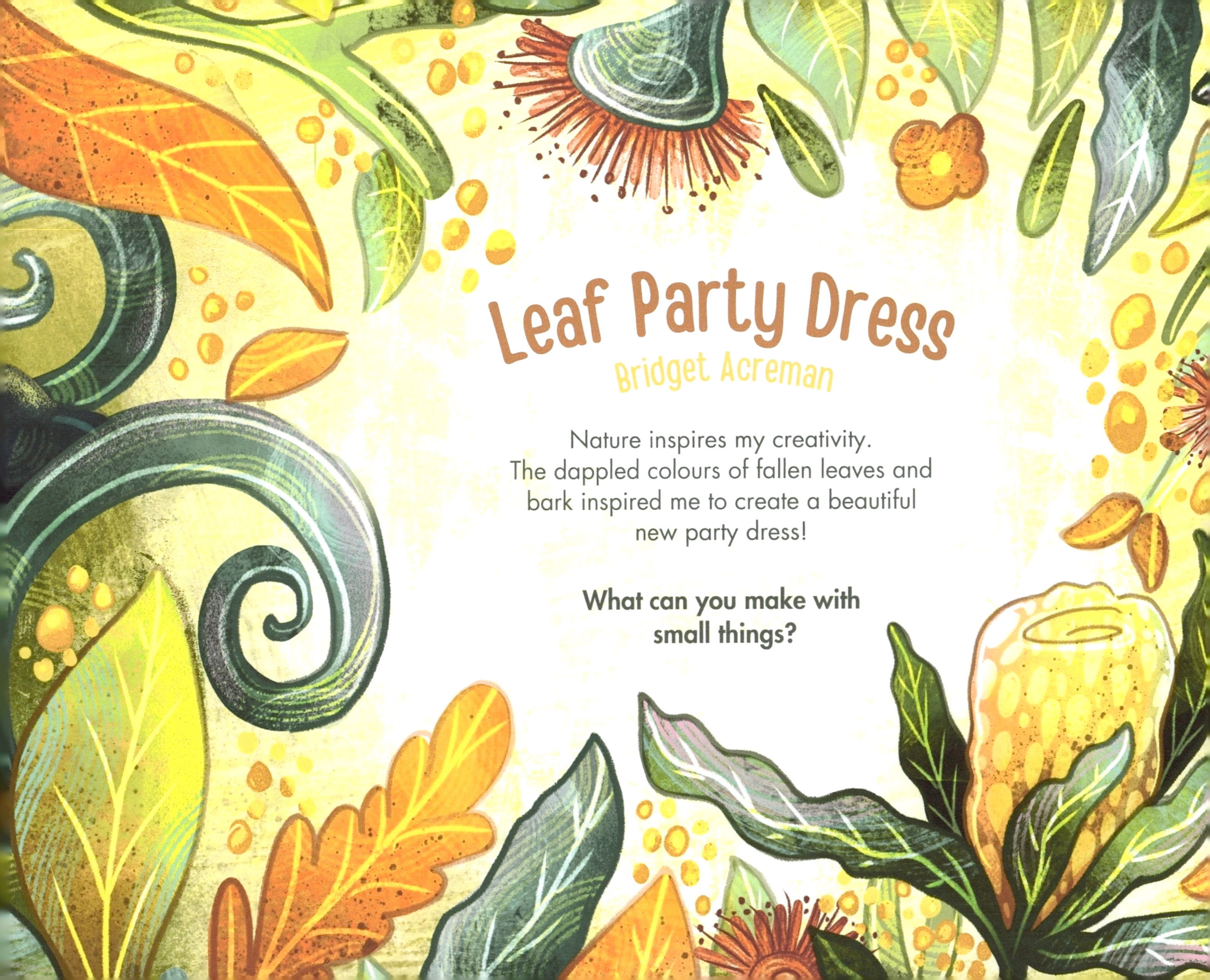

Leaf Party Dress
Bridget Acreman

Nature inspires my creativity.
The dappled colours of fallen leaves and
bark inspired me to create a beautiful
new party dress!

**What can you make with
small things?**

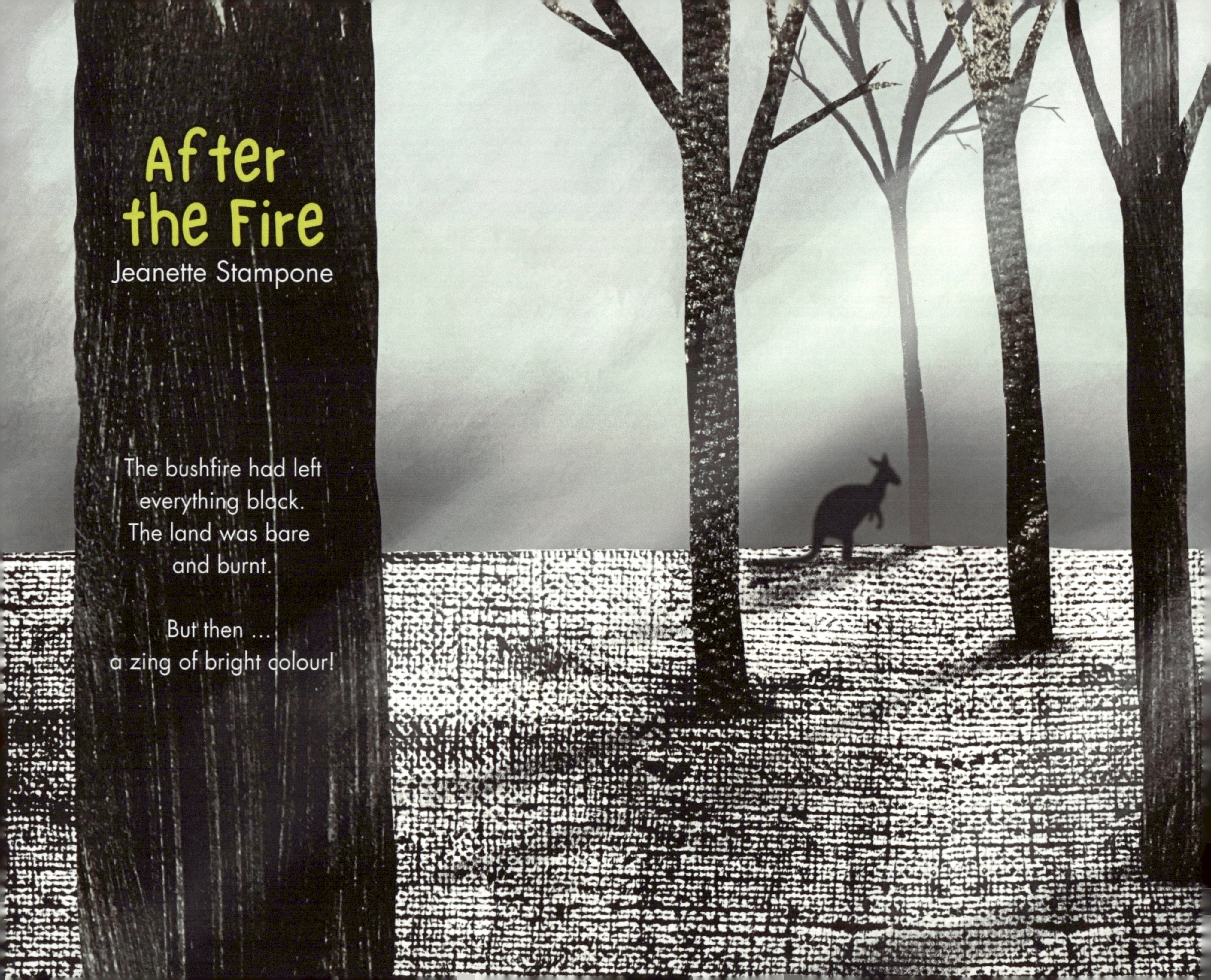

After the Fire

Jeanette Stampone

The bushfire had left
everything black.
The land was bare
and burnt.

But then …
a zing of bright colour!

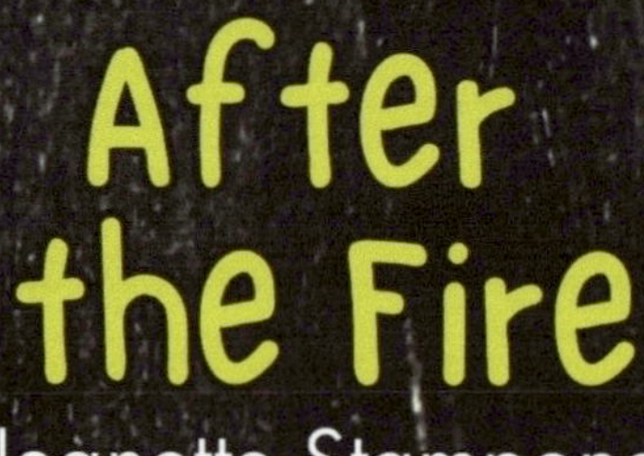

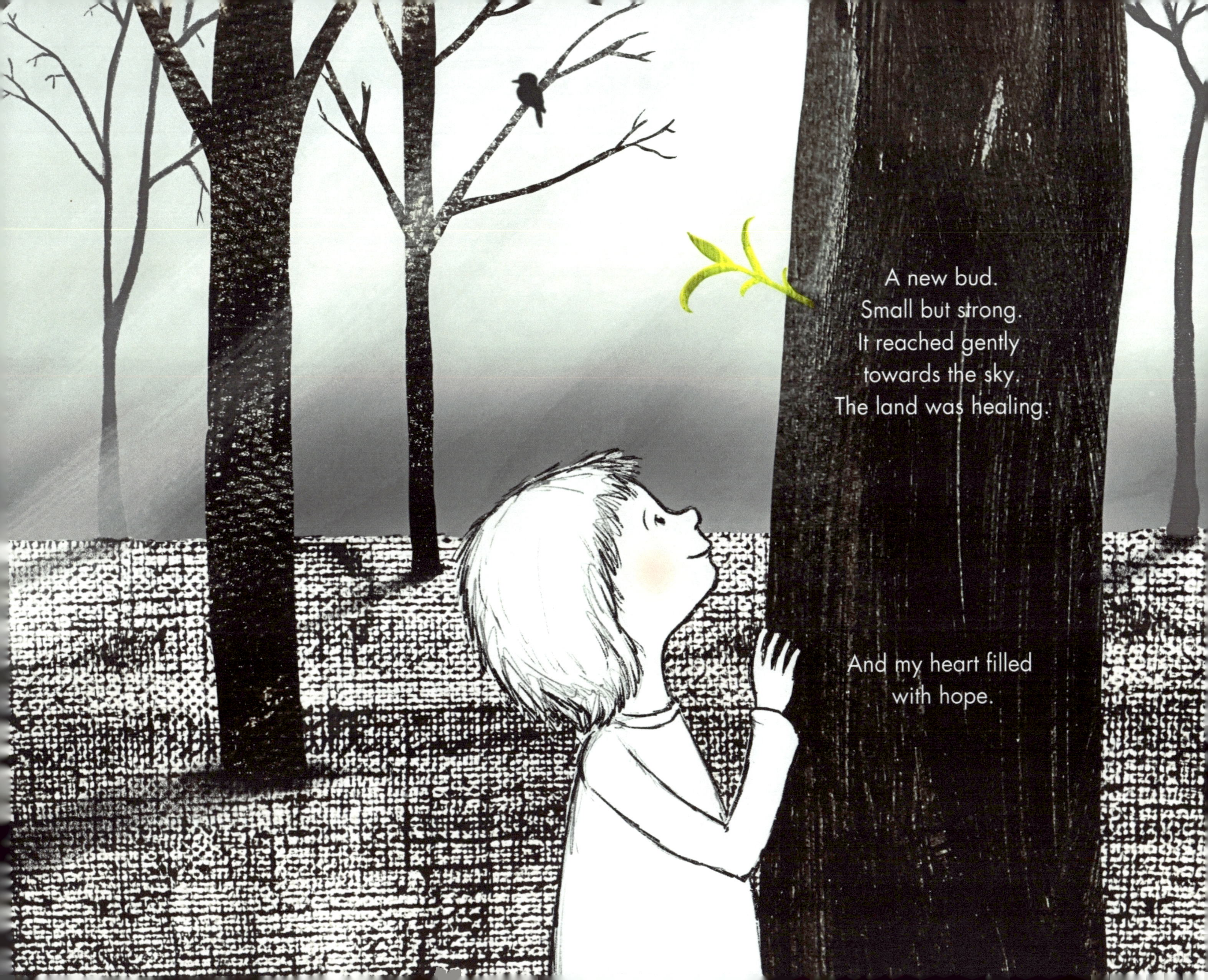

A new bud.
Small but strong.
It reached gently
towards the sky.
The land was healing.

And my heart filled
with hope.

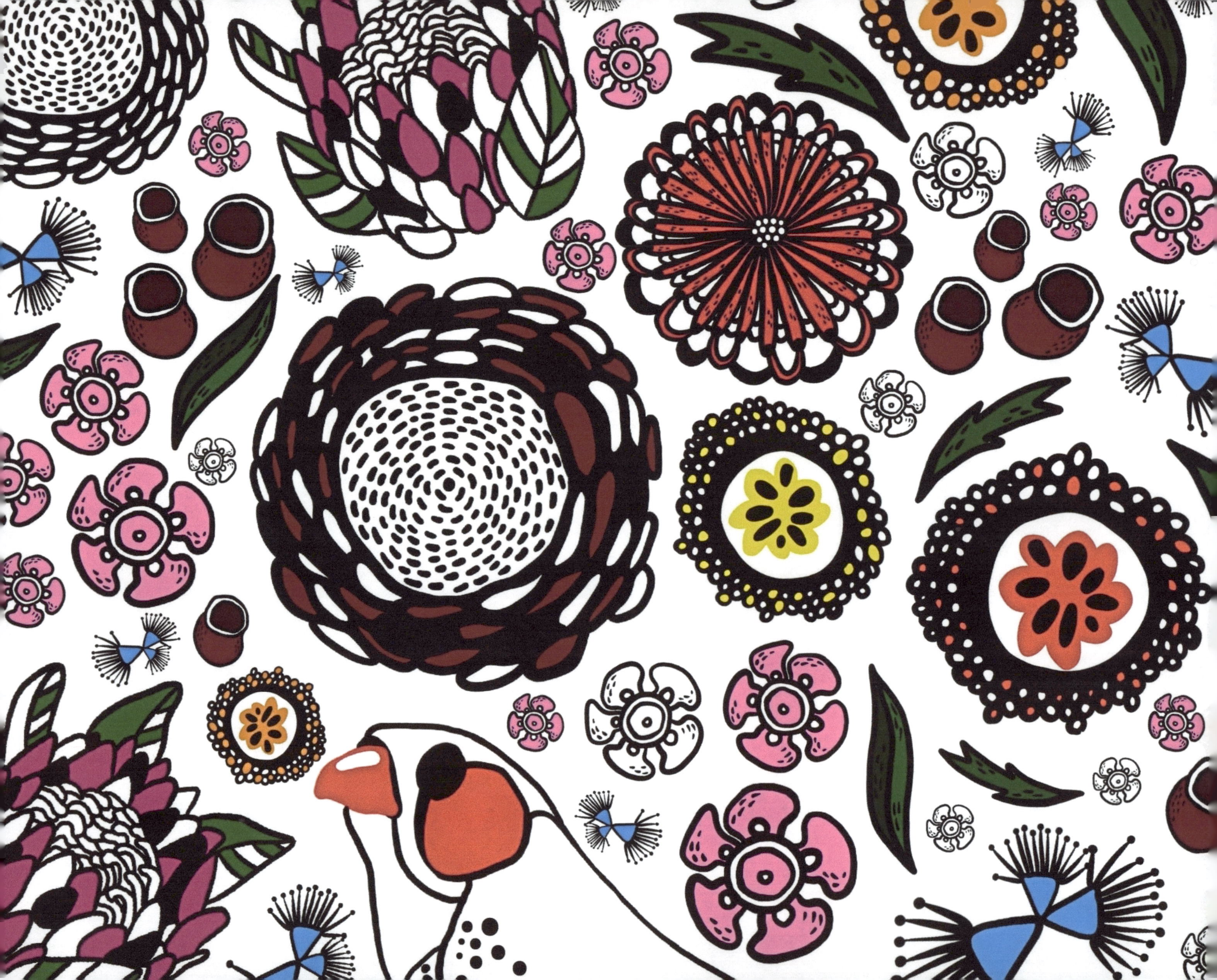

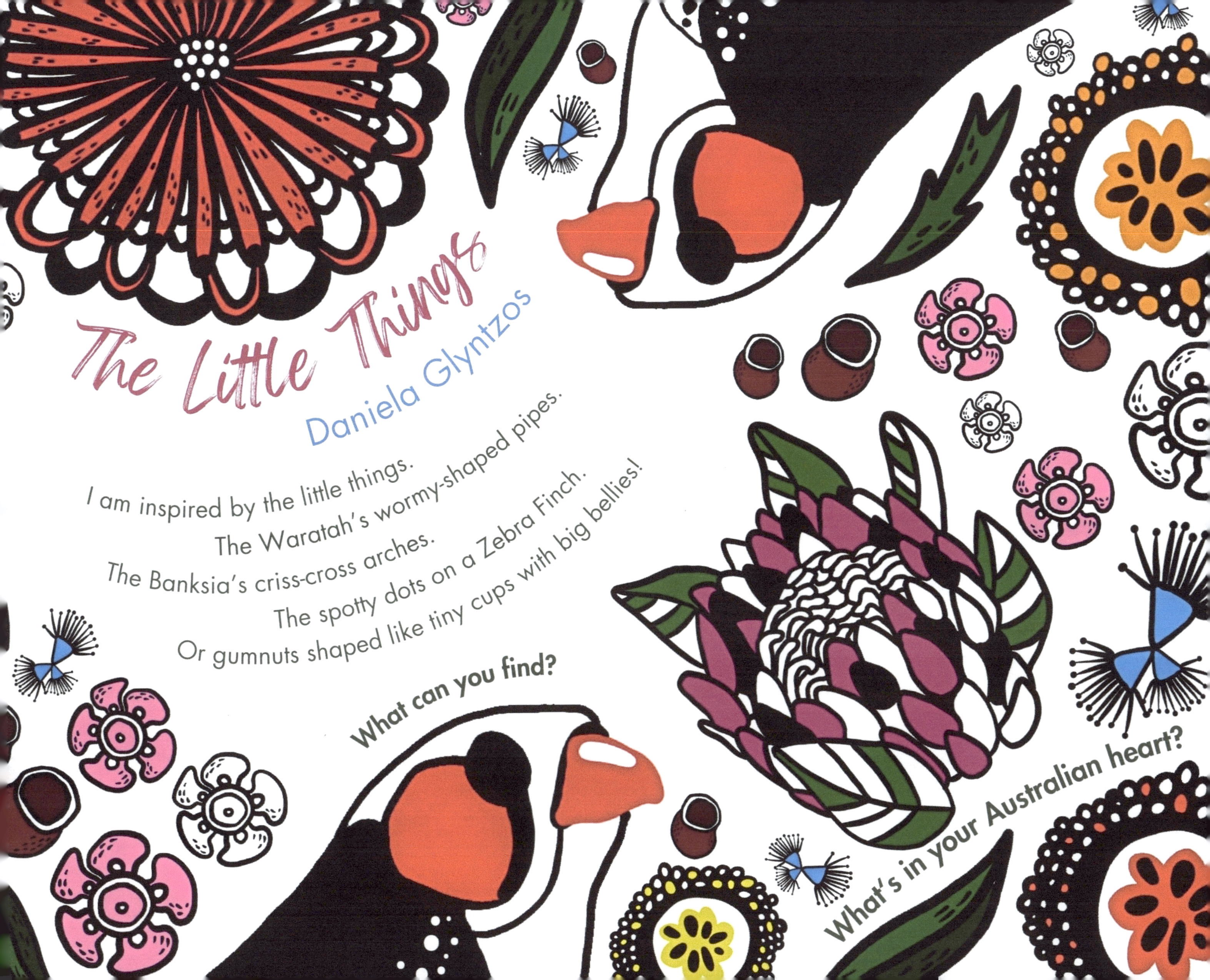

The Little Things

Daniela Glyntzos

I am inspired by the little things.
The Waratah's wormy-shaped pipes.
The Banksia's criss-cross arches.
The spotty dots on a Zebra Finch.
Or gumnuts shaped like tiny cups with big bellies!

What can you find?

What's in your Australian heart?

Jacqui Hewlett

is a pattern designer, author and illustrator who creates unique and intricate illustrations using Adobe Illustrator. Her designs are playful and whimsical. {ponytaildesigns.com}

Alisha Dyer

is a lifelong creative with a passion for art, travel, wildlife, sustainability and inclusivity. Her fine art mediums include oil paint, ink and watercolour. She writes poetry and has a background in graphic design. {@alishamariedyer}

Carla Hoffenberg

is a children's book illustrator, residing in Sydney. She has illustrated two books; *Little Shark Lulu is Sleeping* and *Mia's Glamma*. Carla loves the ocean and is always working on her next children's book. {carlahoffenberg.com}

Kim de Haan

creates illustrations for kids that are warm and optimistic. She mostly works digitally, but likes to incorporate texture and sketchy details to bring in that hand-drawn element. {kimdehaan.com}

Jennifer Horn

is a Brisbane-based illustrator, children's writer, and - like her fellow scrub turkey - new parent. Her fairytale debut picture book, *The Precious Plum* was shortlisted for the 2022 Little Pink Dog's Authorstrator Prize. {jenniferhorn.com.au}

Rachael Robertson

is an author, illustrator and primary school art teacher based in Perth/Boorlo. Her books include *My Amazing Animal Alphabet Alliteration Book* and *What Is It?* She loves to create bright, textured artwork with painted paper collage and by experimenting with different media. {rachaelrobertsoncreates.com.au}

Naomi Eccles-Smith's

creations reflect her love of adventurous quests, deep lore, hopeful themes and fascinating, dynamic characters; her artistic style is reminiscent of 2D animation and Japanese anime, brought to life through Corel Painter's digital mediums. {nrecclessmith.com}

Suzanne Barton

is an author, editor and emerging mixed-media illustrator whose picture books include *Meeka, My Unicorn Farts Glitter* and *My Dad's Weird Beard*. Four new chapter books will be released in 2024. {suzannebarton.org}

Lorraine Miller

is a zoologist and children's author who loves writing about wildlife and nature. Her conservation picture book series is called *The Zookeepers' Quest.*

Jessica Miller

is an illustrator, artist, author and teaching assistant. She enjoys expressing natural forms and animal patterns through her illustrations and digital art. {thezookeepersquest.com}

Rhonda Ooi

is an author and primary school teacher. Her first picture book, *Ned Needs to Build* is due for publication in 2025. {rhondaooi.com.au}

Mel Corrigan

is an illustrator with an architect-trained eye for detail who is passionate about capturing the playfulness and imagination of children. {melcorrigan.com.au}

Michèle Dodd

is a writer, editor and illustrator, living in a leafy suburb in Melbourne. She creates whimsical art pieces and books predominantly with watercolour and pencil. {@micheledoddcreative}

Hannah Friend

is an aspiring children's author and illustrator living in Melbourne. She illustrates digitally, and loves to write fun stories about food, family and friendship. {hannahfriendauthor.com}

Imogen Hartland's

writing and illustrations have featured in a number of literary children's magazines. She uses a variety of different mediums in her artwork, often combining paper collage or printmaking with digital techniques. {imogenhartland.com}

Bridget Acreman

is an illustrator and motion designer from the Central Coast NSW with a background in animation and broadcast design. She hand-draws all her illustrations digitally using a number of tactile texture brushes for a fun organic feel. {strayleaves.com}

Jeanette Stampone

has loved drawing for as long as she can remember. She creates her illustrations digitally, using a sketchy charcoal style, often combined with her own imported painted textures. {jeanettestampone.com}

Daniela Glyntzos

is a contemporary digital artist influenced by society, culture and forms within nature. She loves to work organically, using block colours, stark outlines, and shapes. {danig.com.au}